Radical

Restoration

Finding Your Identity in Christ

D1713380

Dr. Dawn Adkins
Tawnya M. Shaffer

Foreword

Radical Restoration is what occurred in a solitary confinement cell and ended my life of addiction, promiscuity, crime, and hopelessness. I was a 46-time felon and should still be in prison today but by the grace of God and His power, I am free and my purpose is to share the hope and grace that I experienced. As you read this book, you will learn my journey details but instead of remembering my story, my prayer is that you embrace the power of God through each of the following lessons and worksheets.

Radical Restoration is the name of the ministry that I am privileged to run. The ministry includes discipleship homes for women in Florida and Texas that bestow the same knowledge that I experienced and that is in this book. There are several "RRM Snapshots" through the book that will give you a picture of several lives changed by our amazing God and his promises.

Radical Restoration is what God wants for you and your tomorrows. My prayer is that your eyes, ears and hearts will be open to what the Holy Spirit is about to do. If the thoughts that flooded your mind include, "I am too far gone; you don't understand my story; I am hopeless; I have tried everything..." and more, then this book is exactly what you need. God has ordained this moment. How do I know? Because you are holding this book in your hand.

So, here we go. Let's begin and start your Radical Restoration!

Table of Contents

Page 7 .... Why the Dandelion?

Page 9 .... Chapter 1- Surrender

Page 21 .... Chapter 1, Worksheet 1- Salvation

Page 25 .... Chapter 1, Worksheet 2- Baptism

Page 29 .... Chapter 1, Worksheet 3- Making God our Everything

Page 35 ....Chapter 1, Worksheet 4- New Birth, Fresh Start

Page 40 .... RRM Snapshot- Rachael

Page 41 .... Chapter 2- My View of God

Page 53 .... Chapter 2, Worksheet 1- My View of God

Page 57 .... Chapter 2, Worksheet 2- Sins of the Father- Part 1

Page 61 .... Chapter 2, Worksheet 3- Sins of the Father- Part 2

Page 65 .... Chapter 2, Worksheet 4- Sins of the Father- Part 3

Page 69 .... RRM Snapshot- Whitney

Page 71 .... Chapter 3- God's View of Me

Page 85 .... RRM Snapshot- Marianne

Page 87 .... Chapter 3, Worksheet 1- I am His Child

Page 93 .... Chapter 3, Worksheet 2-I am Chosen

Page 99 .... Chapter 3, Worksheet- 3 Identity

Page 105 .... Chapter 3, Worksheet 4- Bride of Christ

Page 111 .... RRM Snapshot – Alyna

Page 113 .... Chapter 4- True Love

Page 125 .... Chapter 4, Worksheet 1- Love Amidst My Mess

Page 131 ....Chap. 4, Worksheet 2- Not a Religion, It's
a Relationship

Page 137 .... Chapter 4, Worksheet 3- No Sin Too Big

Page 141 .. Chap. 4, Worksheet 4- Who or What Owns Your Heart?

Page 145 .... RRM Snapshot – Melanie

Page 147 .... Chapter 5- Worship

Page 157 .... Chapter 5, Worksheet 1- Beyond Church Walls

Page 163 .... Chap. 5, Worksheet 2 Worship Daily-Through our
Actions

Page 167 .... Chapter 5, Worksheet 3- Leaving Old Idols Behind

Page 171 .... Chapter 5, Worksheet 4- Soaking

Page 175 .... RRM Snapshot- Belinda

Page 177 .... Chapter 6- Inner Healing

Page 191 .... Chapter 6, Worksheet -1 Generational Curses

Page 195 .... Chapter 6, Worksheet 2- Counterfeits

Page 199 .... Chap. 6, Worksheet 3- Deliverance from
                                               Strongholds & Oppression

Page 203 .... Chapter 6, Worksheet 4- Healing the Soul

Page 208 .... RRM Snapshot- Jessica

Page 209 .... Chapter 7- Pitiful or Powerful

Page 219 .... Chapter 7, Worksheet 1- Living the Victorious Life

Page 223 .... Chapter 7, Worksheet 2- Powerful Thoughts

Page 229 .... Chapter 7, Worksheet 3- Powerful Words

Page 233 .... RRM Snapshot- Amanda

Page 235 .... Chapter 8- Walk It Out

Page 247 .... Chapter 8, Worksheet 1- Staying True

Page 251 .... Chapter 8, Worksheet 2- Give It Away

Why the Dandelion?

- Did you know the dandelion is one of the hardiest and most recognizable plants?
- Did you know that the dandelion has one of the longest growing seasons?
- Did you know that once a dandelion appears dead and gone (white, cotton and fluffy), that is when it has the most potential?
- Did you know those white fluffy petals have seeds that can travel more than five miles before they create 150-200 new lives?

So, why do I love the dandelion? Because it reminds me of myself. When I was considered hopeless and dead, God used me. He replanted me and gave me new life. That new creation vowed to do God's work and has helped many other dead souls find new life! With Christ, I have power and my joy is extraordinary and others can see Christ in me because of that joy. My goal is to continue with a long growing season, and continue to scatter the truth that set me free, near and all over this world!

Chapter 1

Surrender

~ Salvation ~

~ Baptism ~

~ Making God our Everything ~

~ New Birth, Fresh Start ~

Chapter 1- Surrender

A. Salvation

The first step to a relationship with Jesus Christ may not be what you have been told or taught. Yes, Christ died for each of us over 2000 years ago. Yes, He was tortured, crucified and treated like a criminal, that He was not, because He loved us. Yes, He rose again 3 days later and continues to live today and forever. Because of His actions, the steps to salvation are fairly simple are spelled out in these scriptures:

1. *John 3:16* *"For God so loved the world that he sent his only begotten son that whoever believes in him will not perish but have everlasting life."*

2. *Romans 10:9-10* *"because if you confess with your mouth that Jesus is Lord and believe in your heart that God raised him from the dead, you will be saved. For with the heart one believes and is justified and with the mouth one confesses and is saved."*

3. *Romans 3:22-24* *"the righteousness of God through faith in Jesus Christ for all who believe. For there is no distinction, all have sinned and fall short of the glory of God and are justified by his grace as a gift through the redemption that is in Christ Jesus."*

4. *Ephesians 2:8* *"For by grace you have been saved through faith. And this is not your own doing, it is the gift of God."*

Salvation is a free gift to anyone who chooses. The part that many may miss is truly surrendering your life to Christ. Surrender is defined as an acceptance and a yielding to a higher power. When you recite a prayer that acknowledges your faith in Christ and ask forgiveness for your sins, that is amazing but, a true salvation experience requires a heart change. Words are great, actions are better, and when Christ truly enters your life you will understand this transformation. Your desire to be better for Him will follow. For me personally, I went to the altar many times, said the words many times, went to program after program for my addictions and there was no change. It wasn't until my words joined my heart and included true surrender, did I experience true salvation. And believe me, God will know the difference. God knows the condition of our heart and knows when your decision is genuine or not.

When you experience true salvation, it will include a true surrender. This surrender will have to include changes in your language, relationships, habits and more. When we receive Christ, He abides in us and our body needs to honor him in what we do and say. For many of you, this surrender will require many changes all at once, but you will want to, because of the transformation that you feel within. What are some examples? Basically, discontinuing the actions that your past life told you were ok: smoking, drugs, promiscuous lifestyles, cussing, toxic friendships, and even some of your old wardrobe. Every program I started tried to get me to stop these items but they never worked until I had a real reason to surrender them. For you see Christ loved each of us first and you will want to love Him through the full and complete surrender to Him in your life. Salvation and surrender go hand in hand and you cannot have true salvation without complete surrender.

B. Baptism

Salvation is followed by another act of obedience, the act of baptism. Baptism is being submerged in water and is an outward expression of your new inner faith. It is a symbol of our new commitment to Christ and represents the purification that salvation brings to our hearts. The water is a symbol of cleansing and by being submerged, the old ways are symbolized as being washed away. There is of course nothing special about the water, it is strictly representing what Christ has already done in the life of the believer when they surrendered their life through the act of salvation.

Why do we get baptized? The first reason is that Jesus Christ was baptized and set an example for us by doing so. Jesus' baptism is recorded in **Mark 1:9-11** "In those days, Jesus came from Nazareth of Galilee and was baptized by John in the Jordan. And when he came up out of the water, immediately He saw the heavens being torn open and the Spirit descending on Him like a dove. And a voice came from heaven, "You are my beloved son, with you I am well pleased."

Baptism is an important step of faith because it allows others to see publicly the decision that you have made for Christ privately. It is another step in your faith journey that is very important. Here are a couple more scriptures that talk about the importance of baptism:

1. *Matthew 28:19 "Go therefore and make disciples of all nations, baptizing them in the name of the Father and of the son and of the Holy Spirit."*

2. *Acts 19:5* *"On hearing this, they were baptized in the name of the Lord Jesus."*

3. *Mark 10:39* *"And they said to him, "We are able." And Jesus said to them, "The cup that I drink you will drink, and with the baptism with which I am baptized, you will be baptized."*

You may have been baptized as a baby but if you have made a new decision of salvation at an older age, immersion baptism should be done. There are 3 reasons for this:

1. First, you are now older and are choosing to be baptized, someone else is not making that decision for you.

2. Secondly, immersion was modeled by Christ for us, and in our new life our goal will to be Christ-like in all we do.

3. Third, it will symbolize your fresh change inside to those around you.

Baptism is an outward act of an inward decision and we are commanded and taught to do so by Jesus himself.

C. Making God our Everything

The Bible refers to God as our maker, creator, father, friend, comforter, light, healer, provider, and so much more. He is intended to be our priority and our everything, but that is a foreign concept for most people. The image of God for a large majority of people is an all- powerful deity that is hovering over us and ruling with an iron fist. To consider God as someone that can be close, kind and considerate for many would be questioned and downright laughed at. My prayer is that through these lessons and this book, you will soon realize that our God seeks and longs to be our best friend.

With any relationship, the more time spent together with the other person, increases what you know about each other and helps you to understand each other's ways. A relationship with Jesus is no different. He desires us to seek Him out daily. We need to spend time in His word daily because the Bible is alive and breathing and that is one of the best ways that He talks to us. Bible reading is more than a duty, it is a privilege. The words on those pages are timeless and are a guidebook, a map and a "how-to" for this life on earth. Before reading scripture, ask God to help you understand, and to speak to you directly. You will find in time, that a scripture that you may have read multiple times in the past will teach you a new truth over and over again. The key is to open the Word and read it. Make a plan and stick to it.

Prayer is the other key. Talk to Him a lot. You can talk to God anywhere at any time about anything. Prayer will become automatic the more you spend time doing it. There is no special place or time, the great news is God is always available. He loves it when we come to Him and when we talk to him about anything. Yes, God already knows our thoughts but when we bring them to him we develop a closeness that He desires from us. And communication with our Father is not one sided. We need to be sure to take time to listen for God's voice too. He does speak to his children, but if we are not quiet and still, we may never hear His voice. People may say, God has never spoke to me, but they also rarely have a true quiet time where they sit, Bible open, hands open and simply listen to hear from Him.

One of my most memorable conversations with God happened in solitary confinement. I was desperate and was crying out to God. Yes, you can cry out to Him. You can tell Him that you don't understand and even that you are angry with Him. Honesty is important in all relationships so why not be honest with your heavenly Father? This day I was so tired of it all. I was tired of trying program after program and ending up in prison, addiction and now solitary confinement. I told God, "If you will rescue me, I will commit the rest of my life to helping people like me change their life and live for you."

I was a 46-time felon and should not have been released, but God made a way. He not only got me out of solitary, but out of prison and I ended up starting a home for girls with the same issues as I had struggled with. I have preached in prisons and shared His love with all types of people. I have continued talking and listening to my God since that day in solitary. Don't waste the opportunity to have a relationship with your God.

The content of this chapter can also be called "devotional diligence." We need to strive to be diligent in our devotion to God. He should be in the forefront of our minds every moment of every day. Start your morning with "Hello God." End your day with "thank you for an amazing day in your presence." And in between, make time for his Word, prayer, worship and listening for Him. Your relationship with Christ is the single most important endeavor you will ever take part in. As you progress, you will naturally want more and more time with Him. You will also notice how your life differs when you do not have time with Him. These moments will be like when you thirst for water. You will become to thirst for his teachings and time with Jesus. His word says, *"Draw near to me and I will draw near to you." **James 4:8.***

If God is to be our everything, then He needs to come before anyone and anything in your life!

D. New Birth, Fresh Start

When you accept Christ, it is so important to realize and embrace that you are now a brand-new creation. *2 Corinthians 5:17* says, *"Therefore, if anyone is in Christ, he is a new creation. The old has passed away; behold, the new has come."*

Read that over again. Now read it a 3rd time and put your name in the verse. Claim it. Let it sink deep into your soul and heart. With your surrender, comes the benefit of leaving your old life, old self and old habits behind. Satan will try to discourage you and tell you that your decision was just an emotional one. He will fill your mind with lies and tell you that none of this is true and you are really the same as always.... don't believe it! We will talk a little further in the book about the Holy Spirit. In your journey, you will learn to discern the voice of the Holy Spirit and the voice of the devil. Remember that scripture is always truth and when in doubt turn to it for your answers.

Read the following scripture:

Romans 12:2 *"Do not be conformed to this world, but be transformed by the renewal of your mind, that by testing you may discern what is the will of God, what is good and acceptable and perfect."*

This verse addresses how to walk in our new start. Let's break it down.

1. **Do not be conformed to the world**- don't fall back into your old habits. Don't do what everyone else is doing and do NOT go

back to the old you.

2. **Be transformed by the renewal of your mind-** God has given you the Holy Spirit to change even your thought processes. When you are focused on God and in the Word, you will truly have a transformation of your thought processes. Your thoughts will not be the same as before and when your thoughts change, so do your habits and ultimately your life.

3. **By testing you may discern what the will of God is-** With time, practice and by listening to God- you will know what is right and what is wrong. You will want to please Him the more you know Him.

Step boldly into your new life, your new start and your relationship with an all knowing, all forgiving Father. He wants nothing more than to know you more and more each day. Be purposeful, intentional and ready for the most loving relationship you could ever imagine.

_____

_____

_____

_____

_____

_____

_____

_____

Chapter 1

Worksheet 1

~ Salvation ~

Chapter 1- Worksheet 1
Salvation

It is important to remember your salvation, it is also called your "spiritual birthday." Because this date holds such amazing significance in your life here are a few actions I would like you to take.

1. Write the date and place that you accepted Christ in the front of your Bible.

2. Tell at least 3 people about your decision and how it has changed your life. Write their names here and the date you shared with them. Tell more if you like, who knows you may get to lead them to the Lord through your testimony.

   a. _____ date- _____
   b. _____ date- _____
   c. _____ date- _____

3. Take a few minutes and write a paragraph about your decision to accept Christ. Include details such as, what brought you to the decision, where were you, who prayed with you, how did you feel after? It will be so good to keep this book and look back even years later about that special day. If you accepted Christ a while ago, fell away and have returned to your faith, write that down to and be sure to include what it felt like to be away from God.

_____
_____
_____
_____

_____

_____

_____

_____

_____

_____

_____

_____

_____

_____

_____

_____

_____

_____

- Now take time to think about the sacrifice that Christ gave to save
   you. Then take time to really thank Him for giving his life for
   yours and truly setting you free.

- Read these verses to remind yourself of what He did:
   - Matthew 27:27-
   - Mark 15:15- 32
   - John 19:1-4

Record your thoughts:

_____

_____

_____

_____

_____

_____

_____

_____

Chapter 1

Worksheet 2

~ Baptism ~

Chapter 1
Worksheet 2- Baptism

1. What did you know about baptism before reading this curriculum?

_____

_____

_____

_____

_____

2. How has your view of baptism changed?

_____

_____

_____

_____

_____

3. Write Mark 10:39 here and put your name in place of the word "you".

_____

_____

_____

Now read it aloud 3 times, pray about it and listen to God's voice.

4. Have you been baptized by immersion? If so, write about it here:

_____

_____

_____

_____

_____
_____
_____
_____
_____
_____
_____
_____
_____
_____

5. Look up the following verses about people in the Bible who were baptized:

- Jesus- Matthew 3:13-17
- Simon- Acts 8:9-13
- Saul- Acts 9:18
- An eunuch- Acts 8:38
- The jailer & his family- Acts 10:48
- All types of people- 1 Corinthians 12:13
- Lydia and her family- Acts 16:13-15

What do these verses reveal to you about baptism?

_____
_____
_____
_____

5. Make a plan personally- what is God asking you to do in regards to the act of baptism? Write it out here:

_____
_____
_____
_____

Chapter 1

Worksheet 3

~ Making God our Everything ~

Chapter 1- Worksheet 3
Making God Our Everything

1. The majority of people say "I want to spend more time with God but I am just too busy." With that thought in mind, I want you to do a simple exercise. Fill in the time that you spend on the following activities every day:

Activity	Time Spent Daily
Talking on phone	_____
Texting	_____
Social Media	_____
Television	_____
Eating	_____
Sleeping	_____
Working	_____
Shopping	_____
Devotions	_____
Worship	_____
Prayer	_____

2. Now- take a close look at your results and ask yourself the following questions:

a.   Where can I trim some of my activities that to gain more time with God?

_____

_____

_____

_____

_____

b.   What changes can I make today that would please God?

_____

_____

_____

_____

3. You may have already started to make these changes because you have entered a program that has modeled how to increase your time with God. If that is you, I want you to repeat 1 & 2 but by looking at your life before entering your program. What did this teach you?

_____

_____

_____

_____

_____

_____

4. To truly make God our everything, we often have to re-prioritize and be intentional with our time with God. Life is busy, but don't allow that to crowd God out. Make a plan now to keep Him first in your life.

_____

_____

_____

_____

_____

_____

_____

_____

_____

_____

_____

_____

_____

_____

_____

_____

_____

_____

_____

_____

_____

_____

Chapter 1

Worksheet 4

~ New Birth, Fresh Start ~

Chapter 1- Worksheet 4
New Birth, Fresh Start

1. Read the key verse from this section again. Then we are going to break this down practically.

Romans 12:2 *"Do not be conformed to this world, but be transformed by the renewal of your mind, that by testing you may discern what is the will of God, what is good and acceptable and perfect."*

A. Do not be conformed to the world- don't fall back into your old habits. Don't do what everyone else is doing and do NOT go back to the old you. Make a list of the habits you need to resist and NOT return to:

- _____   - _____
- _____   - _____
- _____   - _____
- _____   - _____

Now list relationships that need to be abolished because they are of the world:

- _____   - _____
- _____   - _____
- _____   - _____
- _____   - _____

B. Be transformed by the renewal of your mind- God has given you the Holy Spirit to change even your thought processes. When you are focused on God and in the Word, you will truly have a transformation of your thought processes. For a while, you may have to verbally rebuke a thought. Look at these examples:

1. Thought- I want a cigarette   Truth- My body is God's home **(1 Cor. 6:19)**
2. Thought- I need a fix   Truth- God is enough **(Isa.12:2)**
3. Thought- I can never do this   Truth- I can do all things with Christ **(Phil.4:13)**

Now you try it. (Remember to ask for help- these will not be automatic at first.) Use your resources around you. Write 5 areas you struggle with the most and a truth that will help you fight the desire to fulfill it.

1. Thought- _____   Truth- _____
2. Thought- _____   Truth- _____
3. Thought- _____   Truth- _____
4. Thought- _____   Truth- _____
5. Thought- _____   Truth- _____

C. By testing you may discern what the will of God is- With time, practice and by listening to God- you will know what is right and what is wrong. You will want to please Him the more you know Him. This one is so rewarding when you first recognize it. If you have already experienced being able to hear God direct you in a situation write about it here.:

_____

_____

_____

_____

_____

_____

_____

_____

_____

_____

_____

_____

If you have not experienced this, it is perfectly fine.... It WILL
happen. Find someone who has and ask them their experience.
Hearing the stories of others will help you to recognize God's voice.
Write their story here:

_____

_____

_____

_____

_____

_____

_____

_____

_____

_____

_____

_____

Take time to pray about your journey. Praise him for how you have
changed. Praise Him for how He is going to continue to work in your
life. Ask Him to help you on your journey. Do not grow
discouraged, draw near to Him and He will draw near to you!

Hi, my name is Rachael and grew up in church. In fact, I was a Pastor's kid. I did not act like a "church girl', in fact, quite the opposite.

I met Pastor Dawn in 2016. I was addicted, suicidal, gay, hurting, and hopeless. I was sick of struggling with addiction. When I first saw Pastor Dawn, she was glowing with a glory that I had never seen before. I could tell she was free and on fire for Jesus. I had honestly never seen anything like the fire of God that burned in this woman, and I had been raised in church! And frankly I haven't seen it since. Then, when I heard her speak, I felt the Holy Spirit give me hope that I still can't explain in words, but this hope made me want to know Him too and give Him my measly gay and addicted life if He wanted it. He did, He wanted me!

Two days after I heard Pastor Dawn speak, I got in the car with her and headed to Radical Restoration Ministries. That's where I felt the love of the Father for the very first time and He continues to hold me in His big arms. I thank God for this ministry. While there I met the Father, and Jesus, and the Holy Spirit and they have changed my whole life. I am a woman on fire now too, burning with the fiery love of God.

After RRM I moved back to Birmingham. The Father has restored my relationships with family, and I purchased my first house. I also earned my Ph.D. I have started Deliverance House Ministries in 2018 as a counseling service and deliverance center for women struggling with addiction and same sex attraction. In 2020, I wrote and published my first book, *Drink Deep: A Manual for More, The Story of the Woman at the Well.*

RRM introduced me to the love of the Father and now I get to introduce others to Him.

Chapter 2

My View of God

~ A Good Father ~
~ A Loving Father ~
~ A Forgiving Father ~
~ What is the Trinity? ~

Chapter 2- My View of God

In this chapter, we are going to explore the character of God. In order to have a healthy relationship with God, you must understand the truths about His character. For many, your view of God is not positive. That view is attached, knowingly or not, to your past authority figures. My prayer is that we can demolish those old views and attachments and give you a new, true and scripture-based view of who God truly is and how you can trust Him and His characteristics. Join me as we explore who God is and why this is a father that will fill those broken places in your soul that you have been longing for.

A. A Good Father

When you hear the word "Father" what reaction do you have? Unfortunately, according to statistics, a majority of you will have a negative response. The reason for that is many earthly fathers have not been true fathers to their children. These dads are absent, abusive, unloving, unkind or all of the above, to their kids. Many kids don't even know who their dads are and suffer the effects of feeling abandoned. There are some of you who grew up in a churched home and knew only rules and legalism (moral and religious law instead of faith and love) from your fathers. Don't be mistaken, both can be harsh and both can leave scars and cause us to cringe when we hear the word father.

So, what happens when someone challenges us to love a heavenly "father?" All of our experiences with our earthly fathers and the negative emotions that we have stuffed down inside for all those years start to surface. Our walls go up and even if you are unaware, the thought of trusting a father and considering a father to be good is resisted at best.

It is time to change all of that. God, the father, is a good father. He does not possess human characteristics or imperfections that many of your earthly fathers did or do. How can you know? How do I trust? It is not easy and is a part of this journey that you are on but we always start with scripture which is all truth. Read the following verses:

1. ***Psalm 103:13*** *"As a father shows compassion to his children, so the Lord shows compassion to those who fear him."*
2. ***1 John 3:1- 3*** *"See what kind of love the Father has given to us, that we should be called children of God; and so, we are. The reason why the world does not know us is that it did not know him, Beloved, we are God's children now, and what we will be has not yet appeared; but we know that when he appears we shall be like him, because we shall see him as he is. And everyone who thus hopes in him purifies himself as he is pure."*
3. ***Luke 11:11- 13*** *"What father among you, if his son asks for a fish, will instead of a fish give him a serpent, or if he asks for an egg will give him a scorpion? If you then, who are evil, know how to give good gifts to your children, how much more will the heavenly Father give the Holy Spirit to those who ask him!"*
4. ***2 Samuel 7:28*** *"And now, O Lord God, you are God, and your words are true, and you have promised this good thing to your servant."*
5. ***Proverbs 3:11-12*** *"My son, do not despise the Lord's discipline or be weary of his reproof, for the Lord reproves him whom he loves, as a father the son in whom he delights."*
6. ***Romans 8:15*** *"For you did not receive the spirit of slavery to fall back into fear, but you have received the Spirit of adoption as sons, by whom we cry, "Abba! Father!""*

So, moving forward in our journey I encourage you to accept and receive the fact that your heavenly Father is good, pure, kind, loving and He longs to embrace you, not only now, but daily and more. Don't allow the sins of your earthly father define the love that awaits you from your Good Father- God! He is a good, good Father.

B. A Loving Father

So, God is a good father, let's build on this. God is a good and loving father. Many people view God as a large figure sitting on a throne glaring down at us, ready to strike us when we do something wrong. Or maybe your view is that God is so angry with me for all that I have done, I fear that He will "give me what I deserve." You are saying, "but you don't understand, there is no way that God still loves me." Let me encourage you that God is not a mad God or a mean father, He loves you despite your mess and He loves you amidst your mess. Yes, He is disappointed when we fail Him, yes, he is saddened when we sin, but God does not want to get even with you or "teach you a lesson." In fact, in scripture it says that Jesus would leave the ninety-nine safe lambs to go and rescue the one lost lamb. *Luke 15:4*

Jesus taught in stories called parables. He did this because it is an easy way for us to understand His teachings. One parable that describes how God is a loving Father is the prodigal son found in *Luke 15:11- 32*. The story describes a son who is given his inheritance at a young age and instead of staying home and working for and honoring his father, he leaves and travels. During his travels, he squanders all of his inheritance. In present day terms, he partied and lived a very promiscuous life until he had no money left. Sound familiar to anyone? He was forced to get a lowly job feeding pigs and ate the pigs' food to survive. That was his low point, can anyone relate? I can, I was there. I was homeless and sold my body and did whatever I could to survive for many years.

Well the prodigal son decided that it would be better to return home and work as a servant for his father than live like he was. So, he did. At home, the father never forgot his lost son. He had another son who stayed, worked and honored him but he longed for the son that he had lost. Scripture says that when the father saw his son returning home *"But while he was yet afar off, his father saw him, and was moved with compassion, and ran and fell on his neck and kissed him." **Luke 15:20**.* He ordered a celebration, put his finest robes on his son and accepted him back.

That is exactly what your loving God wants to do for you. For me, when I had been angry about my circumstances (although they were all a direct result of my actions and disobedience), God told me that I was valuable. He told me in the middle of my solitary confinement cell, "Dawn, you are precious to me and that is why I locked you in this safety deposit box. To protect you and save you." That rocked my world. My God, my heavenly Father loved me enough to save me from myself. And when I was finally ready to "return home" like the prodigal son, He was there with open arms, putting His best robes and rings on me, loving me with no focus on my past choices.

God is a loving father because God is love. His character knows nothing else. The following scriptures are just a few that tell us about the love of God. When you read them, open your heart to the truths within the words.

1. **Psalm 136**:2 *"Oh give thanks unto the God of Gods: for his lovingkindness endureth forever."*
2. **1 John 4:8** *"He that loveth not knoweth not God; for God is love."*
3. **1 John 4:16** *"And we know and have believed the love which God hath in us. God is love; and he that abideth in love abideth in God and God abideth in him."*
4. **1 John 4:7** *"Beloved, let us love one another: for love is of God; and every one that loveth not knoweth not God; for God is love."*

Your Father is so happy that you have surrendered your life and are on this journey to full restoration with Him. I want you to do something for me. Close your eyes. Now imagine the biggest hug that you have ever received. Not a side hug, not a quick hug and release, but a full-on bear hug, long and full. In fact, imagine a child running and jumping into your arms. Once they get to you, they wrap their arms and legs around your torso and they bury their face into your neck. Can you see it? Can you feel it? Child of God, that is the hug that your loving Father wants to give you now and every time you sit at his feet. He loves you! He **LOVES** you! He loves **YOU**! **HE** loves you! Believe it and receive it today!

C. A Forgiving Father

Our Father is good. Our Father is loving. And, our Father is forgiving. This is one characteristic that I am so thankful for. I messed up my life in big ways. Let me summarize for you: a 46-time felon, prostitute, homosexual, bisexual, drug user, drug seller, drug addict, failed my kids, failed multiple marriages, mean to the core, and those are the primary ones. I have been shot, stabbed, raped and beat up. I have been fought, and believe me, I have fought back many times. When people say, "you just won't understand!" My response is, "Try me!" In fact, many times I have called my ministry a "Me too" ministry because I have experienced so much that most times when someone shares their story with me I can say, "me too." I don't share any of this with you for sympathy or to elevate myself in any way. I am where I am today only by the grace of God and His forgiveness.

God's grace and mercy are abounding and are for everyone! Yes, you too! *Romans 3:23 says "For all have sinned and fallen short of the glory of God."* You are not alone. We are all sinners! You, me, people who have sat in church all their lives, and even pastors: all sinners. We all need to know and come to the forgiving Father and ask for his grace. Without the grace of God, we are all hopeless, but with it we are forgiven and can face tomorrow and an eternity with Him.

Let me just speak to those who have just read this and are doubting. This is too good to be true. I am too far gone. Nope, remember my summary above? I am living proof of this powerful mercy. When we ask God to forgive our sins He promises to cast them into the sea.

> **Micah 7:19** *"He will again have compassion on us; he will tread our iniquities under foot; and thou wilt cast all their sins into the depths of the sea."*.

He tells us they are as far as the east is from the west.

> **Psalms 103:12** *"As far as the east is from the west, so far hath he removed our transgressions from us.*

For you see, God forgives and forgets! He does not keep a record of our wrongs to pull back out and remind us of. This Father forgives with a permanent eraser. When we erase with a pencil often there is a trace amount left and we can still see the letters or the impression on the paper. God uses an eraser that leaves NO trace of those indiscretions. Praise God!

Now that God has removed and forgiven our sins, we need to forgive ourselves. Give them to God and truly leave them at his feet. This is easy to write, but not easy to do. It is human nature to beat ourselves up and keep reminding our inner self of our past. As we continue our journey, we will cover this in greater detail and how you can overcome this tendency. For now, accept and embrace the fact that your Father is willing and waiting to forgive and erase the wrongs from your past.

Read the following scriptures on his forgiving nature:

1. **1 John 1:9** *"If we confess our sins, he is faithful and just to forgive us our sins and to cleanse us from all unrighteousness."*
2. **Colossians 1:13- 14** *"He has delivered us from the domain of darkness and transferred us to the kingdom of his beloved Son, in whom we have redemption, the forgiveness of sin."*
3. **Hebrews 10:17- 18** *"I will remember their sins and their lawless deeds no more. Where there is forgiveness of these there is no longer any offering for sin."*

4. *Ephesians 1:7* *"In him we have redemption through his blood, the forgiveness of our trespasses, according to the riches of his grace,"*

a. What is the trinity?

We have talked about our good, loving and forgiving Father so far, this chapter. Before we move on, I think it is important to talk about the trinity and understand it. God is one God but He is in three persons? What, you may ask? Let me break it down for you.

1. **God the Father**- He is the creator of all things. He has been and always will be. He is all powerful, omniscient (all-knowing), and omnipresent (present at all times). He is more powerful than anyone or anything. Yes, He is more powerful than Satan. He knows our todays, tomorrows, and yesterdays. Here are some scriptures about God the Father.
   - *1 Corinthians 8:4* *"Therefore, as to the eating of food offered to idols, we know that "an idol has no real existence," and that "there is no God but one."*
   - *Ephesians 4:6* *"one God and Father of all, who is over all and through all and in all.*
   - *Psalm 135:5* *"for I know that the Lord is great, and that our Lord is above all Gods."*
   - *2 Samuel 7:22* *"Therefore you are great, O Lord God. For there is none like you, and there is no God besides you, according to all that we have heard with our ears."*

2. **God the Son, Jesus**- Jesus was sent by the Father in the form of a man. He entered the world through a human birth. Mary (a chosen virgin) was selected by God to carry the son of God. He was raised as a boy into a man. He learned carpentry skills from his earthy father Joseph. He

started his "training" in the temple at the age of 12. Of course, He knew it all, but He still went through the human steps and training. During his time on earth He experienced pain, emotions, fear and everything that you and I do. The big difference of course is that although a man, He was also perfect because He was also God.

At age 30 (*Luke 3:23*), he started his ministry on earth by selecting and training up disciples that would carry His message to the world after His death. He was questioned and challenged and even tempted by the devil. (*Matthew 4*) At the age of 33 He was arrested, unfairly tried before Pontius Pilate, beaten and tortured and crucified on a cross next to two criminals. Jesus did not deserve any of that treatment. He even asked His Father to, "Take this cup from me" but ultimately, He knew that he had to be crucified to fulfill His Father's plan for us. Through His crucifixion and the shedding of His blood, we are able to be saved from our sins and are given the promise of eternal life in heaven. Then, fulfilling scripture He was raised to life again on the third day and ascended into heaven to be seated by his father.

The fact that Jesus Christ lived as a man assures us that He truly can relate to us and the hardships that we face here on earth. He understands hate, sorrow, jealousy and so many other emotions because He lived through them. Sending Jesus to earth was God's ultimate plan to defeat Satan and His plan to gain ownership over all of our lives. Read these scriptures about Jesus, God the Son.
- *Luke 2:11* *"For unto you is born this day in the city of David, a Savior, who is Christ the Lord."*
- *John 11:35* *"Jesus wept"*
- *Matthew 27:30-31* *"And they spit on him and took the reed and struck him on the head. And*

when they had mocked him. They stripped him of the robe and put on his own clothes on him and led him away to crucify him."

- **Matthew 28:6** *"He is not here, for he has risen, as he said. Come, see the place where he lay."*

- **Isaiah 9:6** *"For to us a child is born, to us a son is given; and the government shall be upon his shoulder, and his name shall be called Wonderful Counselor, Mighty God, Everlasting Father, Prince of Peace."*

3. **God, the Holy Spirit-** The third person of the trinity is the Holy Spirit. When Jesus ascended to heaven, God provided us a helper to be with us. The Holy Spirit is with us here on earth to comfort, direct, guide and fill us with power and hope that is real and tangible. Unfortunately, some churches don't teach a lot on the Holy Spirit. The gifts of the Holy Spirit are true and amazing, but for many congregations and Christians the gifts of tongues, healing and deliverance have been labeled as "taboo" or "out there." Don't make that mistake- there is a reason that God gave us this last part of the trinity. We need His power, His comfort and hope. The Holy Spirit is our gift from God while we still have to exist on this temporary home. Again- we will turn to the Word for truth about the Holy Spirit:

- **John 14:16-17** *"And I will ask the Father, and he will give you another helper, to be with you forever, even the Spirit of truth, whom the world cannot receive, because it neither sees him nor knows him. You know him, for he dwells with you and will be in you."*

- **Mark 1:8** *"I have baptized you with water, but he will baptize you with the Holy Spirit.*

- **Romans 15:13** *"May the God of hope fill you with all joy and peace in believing, so that by* *the power of the Holy Spirit you may abound in hope."*

- **Acts 2:4** *"And they were all filled with the Holy Spirit and began to speak in other tongues as the Spirit gave them utterance."*
- **Acts 2:38** *"And Peter said to them, "Repent and be baptized every one of you in the name of Jesus Christ for the forgiveness of your sins, and you will receive the gift of the Holy Spirit."*

Chapter 2

Worksheet 1

~ My View of God ~

Chapter 2- Worksheet 1
My View of God

For this first worksheet of this chapter, I want you to look inside, be honest and explain below what your view of God was before starting this program. Be detailed. Go!

_____
_____
_____
_____
_____
_____
_____
_____
_____
_____
_____
_____
_____
_____
_____
_____
_____
_____
_____
_____
_____
_____
_____
_____
_____
_____
_____
_____
_____
_____
_____
_____
_____

Next- write how that view has started to change:

_____
_____
_____
_____
_____
_____
_____
_____
_____
_____
_____
_____
_____
_____
_____
_____
_____
_____
_____

Last, but certainly not least, take time to:
1. Pray, and thank God for your transformation so far. Ask Him to continue to reveal himself in new ways every day.
2. Talk to someone about your journey so far. Keeping accountability in this process is essential. Write down who you spoke to and when.

_____
_____
_____
_____
_____
_____
_____

Chapter 2

Worksheet 2

~ Sins of the Father ~
~ Part 1 ~

Chapter 2 – Worksheet 2
Sins of the Father - Part 1

This chapter has focused a lot on the characteristics of God, specifically as a father. To help us continue to heal from past sins of our earthly fathers, and to address generational sins we have been subject to, we will spend the next 2 -3 worksheets to explore these topics through scripture and prayer. To begin we start with the Word. The following scriptures address sins of the father. Read each, pray about what God would have you learn and write your thoughts.

1. *Leviticus 26: 39- 42 -*

   _____
   _____
   _____
   _____
   _____

2. *Deuteronomy 23:2 -*

   _____
   _____
   _____
   _____
   _____

3. *Isaiah 61:4 -*

   _____
   _____
   _____
   _____
   _____

4. *Galatians 3:13-*

   _____
   _____
   _____
   _____

5. *Exodus 20:4-6* -

6. *Nehemiah 9:2* -

7. *1 John 1:9* -

8. *John 20:21-23* -

Close this worksheet in prayer- Ask God to continue to speak to you as He heals these broken places.

Chapter 2

Worksheet 3

~ Sins of the Father ~
~ Part 2 ~

Chapter 2 – Worksheet 3
Sins of the Father - Part 2

Today we do some major soul seeking and internal honesty. I need you to brainstorm any and all emotional hurts from your past. When you write them, write the person, the hurt and approximately when it happened. Start with prayer and then let the thoughts come- the key is brainstorm! Here is a list of some examples to get you going. God is doing some amazing transformations in your life! Blessings as you pour out onto this page.

Examples of Generational Sin

Abandonment/Rejection	Fear/Anxiety/Worry
Control/Manipulation	Addiction
Shame/Unworthiness	Abuse/Victim
Anger/Rage/Violence	Poverty
Occult/Idolatry	Lawlessness/Rebellion
Sexual Sins/Illegitimacy	Pride/Stubbornness

_____
_____
_____
_____
_____
_____
_____
_____
_____
_____
_____
_____
_____

Use the back or a second page if you need more space.

Chapter 2

Worksheet 4

~ Sins of the Father ~
~ Part 3 ~

Chapter 2 – Worksheet 4
Sins of the Father - Part 3

Today, we leave all the hurt behind- FOR GOOD. This next step can be done alone, but I strongly encourage you to do it with another person. The emotions will run high, that is ok. Another person will help you to stay focused and not miss any steps. Remember, accountability is key! So, this is how to proceed. **For each** of the hurts you listed above, you are going to do the following steps:

1. Pray the prayer (steps 1-6) below by inserting the appropriate names and sins into the spaces.
2. Pray the ministry paragraph for each person that caused hurt in your life.
3. Be sure to say each word- they hold power.

Note- You may have to do this over more than one sitting. Use your judgement, this is a freeing but also a very emotional exercise.

Prayer

1. Lord, I confess the sins of my fathers and my own sin of

_____.

2. I release and forgive my ancestors and parents for these sins of _____ and the curses involved, and how their sin affected my life by _____.

3. I ask You to forgive me for this sin in my own life and how I have participated in it by _____.

4. I forgive myself for my involvement and for any guilt, shame, self-rejection (any other emotions) I may have carried.

5. I renounce any more involvement with these sins and curses of _____ and BREAK their power in my life, and my descendants through the redemptive work of Christ on the Cross. I won't put up with them anymore! AMEN

6. I receive _____.

RRM Snapshot .... Meet Whitney ~

After 18 years of addiction and on the brink of losing my son, I finally cried out to God. I have always believed in God but never had a true relationship. I went to church a lot and experienced a lot of religion but nothing about a relationship with Jesus.

My dad was heavy in an addiction to crack and I experienced a lot of disappointment in our relationship. I had ADD at a young age and was put on medication. I believe this is what started my addiction to drugs at the age of 14. The older I got, the worse the drugs got. I continued to go to church with my parents but I felt like an outcast and was full of shame and secrets. I bounced between guys all the time and took whatever drug they did. The lack of validation that I never received from my dad led to my addiction to men. I was falsely seeking the love and validation that I really needed from God.

I got pregnant at the age of 19 and had my son. I smoked weed through my pregnancy because I didn't feel it was "that bad." I resumed my drug habits right after delivery. I often bought them off the street because I couldn't pass a drug test for my ADD drugs. Since I was an adult, my dad and I started doing drugs together. To me, this was finally "approval from him" that I had so deeply wanted. I eventually did it all and often had a needle in my arm.

After years of the same cycles, I hit a wall. I was 99 pounds, strung out, in an abusive relationship, no job and had lost my son. I became the person I never thought I would be.... I was hopeless!

I started a 4-year span of rehab after rehab and then relapse after relapse. I gained head knowledge but never found healing. I would "come to Christ" and get baptized again and again but with no permanent change.

God led me to Radical Restoration and I remember standing at the altar and crying out to God. He told me, "Whitney you are beautiful and I have always pursued you." I received a true heart transplant. I truly felt loved!

God has restored my relationship with my family and son. My dad has been healed from his addiction. I am healed and whole. I am now ministering to other single mothers and sharing His love.

Chapter 3

God's View of Me

~ I am His Child ~

~ I am Chosen ~

~ Identity ~

~ Bride of Christ ~

Chapter 3- God's View of Me

Now that we have looked closely into your view of God, we are going to turn it around and look at His view of us. Did you just cringe? Are you fearful of what He feels about and towards you? I think you may be pleasantly surprised at how your Heavenly Father loves and accepts you. Let's get started!

A. I am His child

There is a reason that God is called our "Heavenly Father" that is just one of his names and actions. Let's take a look at his Word. Look up the following verses and see what they have to say concerning you as His child.

1. Deuteronomy 32:6 -

   _____

2. Malachi 2:10 -

   _____

3. Matthew 23:9-

   _____

4. 1 Corinthians 8:6-

   _____

5. Ephesians 4:6-

   _____

6. Hebrews 12:9-

   _____

7. Matthew 7:11-

   _____

8. Romans 8:15 -

   _____

God is not only our creator but He is our Father, which makes us His children. He desires a closeness with you like a healthy earthly father does with his child. We have already talked about the fact that not all of our earthly relationships are "normal" and "healthy", but those that have experienced a good relationship with their parents, can tell you that spending time together is precious and essential for a close and intimate relationship.

For years, I did not experience a close, normal or loving family experience because of my poor choices from a young age. I made decisions that pushed my parents away and when I was blessed with my children, I was too promiscuous, high or homeless to develop any type of healthy relationships with them. So, you may ask how are you qualified to teach this? Because, God has blessed me in two ways. First, He has shown me what a loving Father is and what it means to be wanted and loved. Second, He has given me close friends that have demonstrated to me what a family of Christian legacy looks like. These examples have challenged me to work on my relationships with my earthly family and wow, has God come through and blessed the healing process (I will share more on this as we go through this curriculum). So, let's talk about what I have learned and what I challenge you with as God continues to restore you!

How do I develop the closeness that God desires with me? One of the first ways to accomplish is to **press into His presence**. Time is one component of that, of course, but also being intentional. God is always available, it is always on us when we don't give Him first priority. Our lives are crazy, our time is divided between so many demands, but when we don't prioritize God in our daily schedule, we suffer. "Pressing in" is an action verb and implies an intentional, regular, and quality time together. Putting Him first, and keeping Him in the forefront of our mind through all of our interactions will become automatic, the more that you "press in."

As you learn to press in, you will also learn to **pursue Him** with a new passion like never before. Once I found Jesus and fell deeply in love with Him, I pursued Him like he was water or food to my existence. In *Psalm 42:1*, David describes this feeling as he wrote, *"As the deer pants for streams of water, so my soul pants for you, my God."* As I drew closer, I learned to hear from Him, and He would tell me, "Dawn, you are my favorite." I have never stopped believing that to this day. I know with all certainty that I am His favorite! People still laugh at me but I know it is the truth. And, over the years of Radical Restoration Ministries I have taught all my girls that they are His favorite too. But, unless you are pressing in and pursuing Him, you may not believe that. But, please believe me, you are His favorite too- you are His child, His favorite!!!

One barrier to the last two steps is **going past the facts**. Like me, you may have been in program after program. You have done the 10 steps, the 12 steps and worked curriculum after curriculum. I even went to the altar over and over, said the words, but there was one problem with all of these. They were based on facts, man's ideas and writings. Are these bad? No, and they work for a lot of people. BUT, they are not God. Head decisions are not heart decisions. Once we simplify and say yes to God, a true surrender, embrace that we are His child, we will need His love more than any facts. For you see the one program that will never fail is one step... saying yes to Jesus!

So, as you **press in**, **pursue him, go pass the facts** you will automatically go from **knowing of Him and truly knowing Him**. You are His child, He is your father and He is real! As you spend intimate time together, open yourself to Him, He will open up to you. His characteristics will no longer be words on a page. He will become a tangible presence in your daily life. You will see Him in answered prayers, people He puts in your path and so much more. Jesus is all around us, we just often fail to see Him because we don't know Him the way he designed us to know Him. *Hebrews 10:22* says, *"let us draw near to God with a sincere heart and with the full assurance that faith brings, having our hearts sprinkled to cleanse us from a guilty conscience and having our bodies washed with pure water."*

B. I am chosen

For many people, being chosen by someone, is unfamiliar and the concept of the one, all powerful God choosing you may seem utterly ridiculous. But, it is not. Christ chooses each of us, regardless of our past, present, and yes, even our future. He desires us to reciprocate and choose Him, but for some who turn away from God, He still chooses and pursues each of us.

Beloved identity is one of my favorite topics to teach on because I understand the transformation of feeling unloved by everyone to being cherished by "the One." Read that sentence over again, and really let it sink it!! When I talk about beloved identity the primary message is to convey both knowing and understanding the depth of love He has for you. Beloved means "dearly loved; a much-loved person." In scripture one of the ways our Lord is depicted is as the Good Shepherd who cares for his sheep (yep, that is us, and for the record, sheep aren't the brightest creatures on this planet.) Take a few minutes and read *Luke 15:3-7*. This scripture depicts Christ's great love for us in the form of a parable or story. He tells how a good shepherd will leave the ninety-nine he has, to find the one lost sheep. We are each valuable to Him and He seeks out each of us.

I first experienced this deep love when I was in solitary confinement. I was facing a very long sentence and had no hope. As I sat there alone, with no chance of parole, I decided to talk to God. I told him, "God, if you are there, and if you are real, I will make you a deal. If you get me out of here, I will dedicate my life to helping women just like me." I heard the voice of God in such a real and tangible way. His reply was, "I put you here because you are valuable to me. And what does one do with valuables? You lock them in a safety deposit box. You are here because you are valuable to me." I knew right then, that my life was forever changed, I was chosen and loved! Miraculously, I was released, pardoned and I never forgot my conversation with God. It was the first of many talks and I kept my part of the deal, just like He had for me.

To look deeper at being God's beloved, we will be looking deeper into Song of Solomon at the end of this chapter but to get us started look up these verses:

1. Song of Solomon 2:10

_____

_____

2. Song of Solomon 2:16

_____

_____

3. Song of Solomon 7:10

_____

4. Deuteronomy 33:12

_____

_____

Do you see a trend here? You are truly His beloved- cared for deeply and fully and He will continue to seek you out until He has your full devotion. Another key point in understanding that you are chosen, is that **Christ would have died just for you.** If you were the only one that He could save by dying on the cross, He would have still done it. He is fully and completely devoted to you, to the point of death. I think early on I believed this but the comprehension of the depth of His love for me has been a process. Partly because our human brains cannot fathom the depth of His love. Read ***Romans 8:39*** for a little more info about the depth of His love. Christ died for you, He died for us all. Even the worst of the worst humans on the earth, yes God **chose** to die the that person too. The last part of being chosen is that He has **appointed you for a divine purpose**. Every child of God is designed for a reason, a task, a calling to support the kingdom of God. So many individuals struggle with a lack of purpose and feel hopeless. Once they can get in touch with God, connect with Him intimately, He will reveal the purpose that he has designed you for.

C. Identity

A barrier to accepting the truths of God's view of us is wrapped intricately in our identities. Every human battles with true versus false identities. Our self-perception is developed by our experiences, interactions and environment. The problem with that, is many of those are not positive for us. Most people, when honest, can testify that either their home life, school experiences, work environment, or a combination of all three have made them feel bad about themselves. Satan wants nothing better than to feed us these lies about our identity. A verse that I learned early in my Christian relationship was **1 Peter 5:8**. It says, ***"Stay alert! Watch out for your great enemy, the devil prowls around like a roaring lion, looking for someone to devour." NLT***. This verse holds so much truth for us. The devil is working so hard to destroy us and keep us from our intended relationship with our Heavenly Father. Our self-image is easy access for him. Here are some examples:

Satan's lie:

1. You are not good enough
2. You have sinned too much
3. You are condemned
4. You are unworthy

Now look at the truth:

God's truths:

1. You are beautifully made
2. All your sins are forgiven
3. You are accepted
4. You are chosen

Satan's goal is to take these falsehoods, embed them deep within us so they become our identity. If the father of lies (John 8:44) can convince us that we are not "good enough", he can use these false identities to keep us from Christ. So, if we listen to these lies, these are the type of identities that we may have accepted:

1. Dirty/ unworthy
2. Addict
3. Homosexual
4. Victim
5. Useless
6. Abandoned
7. Broken
8. Prisoner
9. Unwanted
10. Invaluable

Now, let me remind you the title of this chapter, *God's view of you*. And I can assure you that His view of you does not include any of these! In our worksheets following this chapter, we are going to take some time to explore what your current identities are, and to be sure they are in line with who Christ says you are. What you have to remember is God is truth and Satan is deceit. God is, and always will be, more powerful than Satan. God has the power to break all of these falsehoods and truly open you to not only hear, but receive and believe your identity in Christ. Our God is a chain breaker, a restorer, and a freedom giver. He holds your identity, and once you can embrace that, you will walk forever in that freedom!

D. Bride of Christ

One of the most intimate relationships in this world, is the relationship between a husband and a wife, so what does it tell you that God calls us, you and me, His bride? Yes, that is what he thinks of you, and how He loves you. Through scripture Jesus is called the bridegroom and we, the church, are called His bride.

Read *Isaiah 62:5* with me: *"As a young man marries a maiden, so will your sons marry you; as a bridegroom rejoices over his bride, so will your God rejoice over you."*

Now read *Revelation 19:7* *"Let us rejoice and be glad and give him glory! For the wedding of the Lamb has come, and his bride has made herself ready."*

What an incredible honor! The God of this universe calls us His bride! Some of you have just started to think, "Not me, I am not pure enough to be His bride." Aha, gotcha! That is a false identity surfacing! See how this all works together. We ARE... ALL... HIS...BRIDE! God loves us with the same love as a groom does for his bride on their wedding day. When you accepted Christ, you became a brand-new being. In the verse *2 Corinthians 5:17* (One of my favorites) we are assured of this. It says, *"Therefore if anyone is in Christ, the new creation has come. The old has gone and the new is here."*

Song of Solomon is probably the most avoided and most misunderstood book of the Bible. But, for me, and soon for each of you reading this curriculum, it will become your personal favorite. Why? Because it is an actual love letter to us from God. He is addressing his personal love journey with His beloved bride. And His beloved, the maiden is on a journey to understand the intimacy that God desires with us. The book is a description of her journey as she gets to know the bridegroom's nature and His love for her. Read this verse from *Song of Solomon 4:9*: *"You have stolen my heart, my sister, my bride; you have stolen my heart with one glance of your eyes, with one jewel of your necklace."*

This is just one example of many verses addressing His deep love for you. I hope that this chapter has helped you to truly embrace that you are His child, chosen by God, beautiful, and intimately loved. Don't ever again allow the lies of this world to tell you otherwise! His view of you is entirely positive, full of acceptance and love like you have never experienced before. Allow these truths to soak over you. Allow yourself to be loved with His immeasurable and unconditional love today!

It is never too late to be set free and truly loved! At the age of 60 I have been redeemed by the blood of Jesus and now know true love!

For roughly 40 years and growing up in church I knew God in my head but not in my heart. I have had 2 failed marriages and many failed relationships. I yearned for love so much I would look for it anywhere. This unmet need led to my addictions.

I began using opioids after a neck surgery. After taking the pills I felt no pain and had energy and clarity. They dulled all the pain in my life. The longer I took them, the less effect they had so I took more and more. I even stole pills from my addicted mother. I checked into a 30-day rehab center and thought I was healed.

After a brief time staying clean I turned to alcohol with the false belief that my only addiction was pills. I hid my drinking more and more. I got a DUI and all the shame that goes with it. I even kept a breathalyzer in my car to keep tabs on how much I could get away with. Before long I was drinking 24/7. I lost my job, car and family. After 6 months, I was out of money and needed the alcohol. I was desperate and hopeless.

On December 9, 2019, my son and sister asked if I was ready to make a change. I checked into the hospital to detox safely and then entered Radical Restoration program for women. Jesus entered my life and showed me what true love really looks like. He loves me so much and is all I will ever need. Drugs, alcohol or men can't begin to compare to the peace, love and joy that Jesus brings to my life.

I am a new creation and you can be too! I pray that as you read this book you will find the love of Jesus like I have!

Chapter 3

Worksheet 1

~ I am His Child ~

Chapter 3 – Worksheet 1

I am His Child

Let's take a closer look at how we know we are a child of God. Here are the verses you looked up. I want you to look them up again and this time write what you learned from each:

1. Deuteronomy32:6

   _____

   _____

   _____

   _____

2. Malachi 2:10-

   _____

   _____

   _____

3. Matthew 23:9 -

   _____

   _____

   _____

   _____

4. 1 Corinthians 8:6 -

   _____

   _____

   _____

   _____

5. Ephesians 4:6 -

   _____

_____

_____

_____

6. Hebrews 12:9 -

_____

_____

_____

7. Matthew 7:11 -

_____

_____

_____

8. Romans 8:15 -

_____

_____

_____

_____

We have talked about pressing in and pursuing God in this chapter- Let's make a plan on how you plan on doing that. Be sure to include prayer time, scripture time and even journaling. Also, quiet time is essential so you have time to hear from God. Write your plan below and then share your plan with someone who will hold you accountable. _____

_____

_____

_____

_____

_____

_____

_____

_____

_____

_____

_____

_____

_____

_____

_____

_____

_____

_____

_____

_____

_____

Chapter 3

Worksheet 2

~ I am Chosen ~

Chapter 3 – Worksheet 2

I am Chosen

1. Think back anytime in your life to an occasion when you were chosen for something positive. Write out your experience here. How did that make you feel?

_____

_____

_____

_____

_____

_____

_____

_____

2. Now, compare that to learning that you are chosen by your Heavenly Father. Write your feelings here:

_____

_____

_____

_____

_____

_____

_____

_____

_____

3. Look up the following verses again:
   Song of Solomon 2:10-

   _____

   _____

   Song of Solomon 2:16 -

   _____

   _____

   Song of Solomon 7:10 -

   _____

   _____

   Deuteronomy 33:12 -

   _____

   _____

4. How do these emphasize to you that you are chosen by
   God? _____

   _____

   _____

   _____

5. Write out Romans 8:39:

   _____

   _____

   _____

   _____

Now take a few minutes to really study that passage- allow the
truth to sink in.

6. You are chosen for a divine purpose, God has a plan and a purpose for your life. We are all here to help to advance the kingdom of God. Read **Romans 12:4-8**. Write the different gifts that this scripture lists:

a. _____

b. _____

c. _____

d. _____

e. _____

f. _____

g. _____

h. _____

As you progress into the curriculum, pray that God will reveal to you what gift He has given you. Maybe you already know. Take a few minutes to pray about these gifts. Write below what God reveals to you.

_____

_____

_____

_____

_____

_____

_____

_____

_____

_____

Chapter 3

Worksheet 3

~ Identity ~

Chapter 3 – Worksheet 3

Identity

Ok, time to get honest again. Before we start this section, take some time to pray, quiet your heart and ask God to guide you in these exercises.

First, write down 5 words that described you before you found Jesus:

1. _____

2. _____

3. _____

4. _____

5. _____

With these adjectives of yourself, how did you describe yourself?

_____

_____

_____

_____

_____

_____

_____

_____

Do you see false identities or lies from Satan in the words on your list? List the lies-

1. _____

2. _____

3. _____

4. _____

5. _____

Now- write 5 words that describe yourself since you found Jesus and through God's eyes:

• _____

• _____

• _____

• _____

• _____

Here is the list of the false identities from our lesson- Write a true identity by each false identity.

Dirty/ unworthy   – _____

Addict   – _____

Homosexual   – _____

Victim   – _____

Useless   – _____

Abandoned   – _____

Broken   – _____

Prisoner   – _____

Let's take what we learned- write about your new identity in Christ below. Be honest and transparent. Remember all that you have been taught and leave the past and lies behind.

_____

_____

_____

_____

_____

_____

_____

_____

_____

_____

_____

_____

_____

_____

_____

_____

_____

_____

_____

_____

_____

_____

_____

_____

_____

_____

_____

_____

Chapter 3

Worksheet 4

~ Bride of Christ ~

Chapter 3 – Worksheet 4
Bride of Christ

1. What do you think about being the bride of Christ? Is this truth new to you?

_____

_____

_____

_____

_____

2. Why do you think God chose this relationship to describe His love for you?

_____

_____

_____

_____

_____

_____

3. For most of this worksheet we are going to do something different. We are going to read through the Song of Solomon. Before reading it, please don't expect to understand it all completely. God will reveal to you what He wants you to hear. I want you to do a few tasks as you read:

- Highlight the word **beloved** every time you see it.
- Highlight the word **love** every time you see it.

- Write your thoughts below as God reveals them to you.
- Discuss your thoughts with someone when you are done.

_____

_____

_____

_____

_____

_____

_____

_____

_____

_____

_____

_____

_____

RRM Snapshot .... Meet Alyna ~

I grew up in a dysfunctional environment. Watching others in their addictions sparked my curiosity. At age eleven, I started using drugs. For thirteen years, I spiraled out of control, doing every drug I could find including psychotropic ones.

The vicious cycles of my addiction took me through abuse, dysfunction, homelessness and multiple overdoses. I bounced from one dealer to another. I was so overcome with pain and shame I began selling my body for meth. I was seeking validation and love in all the wrong places. I was desperate to fill a void but instead continued to feed the rage and the anger that resided in my soul. After multiple therapists and incarcerations, I finally hit my rock bottom and that is where I found my Rock- Jesus! I was hopeless and ready to die. I fell on my knees and called out to God, and I didn't even know if there was a God but in desperation I cried out. He sent me to a lady to pray for me.

At that meeting, there was a presence that filled the room and I knew it was God. I felt hot oil flowing through my body like fire. God told me that I was His and how much He loved me. He lifted a veil and revealed to me all the moments of my life where He had been, even in the darkest times when I felt unloved, disgusting, filthy, lonely and worthless.... He was there with me!

After that, I entered Radical Restoration home and I have learned to walk in my beloved identity. All my chains are broken. I am learning to be the powerful woman of God that he created me to be. I am so thankful that at age 24, love came down and rescued me. No drug has ever made me feel the way that Jesus does. My entire family has been restored, healed and set free. I get to share the love of God and what he continuously doing in and through me. I am forever changed and get to be my authentic self, a daughter of the King!

Chapter 4
True Love

~ Love Amidst my Mess ~

~ Not a Religion, it's a Relationship ~

~ No Sin Too Big ~

~ Who or What Owns Your Heart ~

Lesson 4- True Love

We have explored true surrender, our view of God, and God's view of us. Love has already been a big part of our conversations because to discuss God, it is hard to do so without involving love. This chapter will dig even deeper into some of the practical aspects of God's love and how it manifests in your process; your past and your future. Before my solitary confinement transformation, I did not believe a love like his existed but I testify every day to how I see the handprint of His love on my journey. Let's go!

A. Loved amidst my mess

Think back to the lowest point of your life, I know it may not be easy but we won't stay there. Close your eyes and visualize the place, the smell, the pain. Now look around because Jesus was there with you then and now. I know you are thinking, no way! Jesus would never go there. But I disagree. The Bible is full of examples of Jesus going to the prostitutes, tax collectors, pagans, demons possessed and lepers. Take a minute to look up the following verses: *Matthew 9:12, Mark 2:17, Luke 5:31.* They are all an account of the same teaching of Jesus to his disciples and Jesus tells them, *"It is not the healthy that need a doctor but the sick."* Jesus was there with you in all your mistakes, waiting and ready for you to return to Him. He is your father remember, and He has been waiting for His child to run back into his arms.

He loved you in your mess- before you even thought about this day. *Romans 5:8* affirms that by saying, *"But God demonstrates his own love for us in this. While we were still sinners, Christ died for us."* Have you ever truly tried to imagine the enormity of God's love for the world. I mean really try to envision it. Our human minds cannot fathom it, and when I think what we must sound like to him on a daily basis; "God do this" "God I need that." "Help me God" ... Boy He is a God of patience too!

Remember in the last chapter we discussed how Jesus would leave the ninety-nine safe lambs for the one lost lamb. - *Matt. 18:12, Luke 15:1-7* recounts this story. There is another parable, the parable of the lost coin found in *Luke 15:8-10* that holds the same truth. Take a minute to pause and read that parable too. Jesus is actively looking and waiting for you while you are lost. If He didn't love you, would He do this? NO. He would probably act like any human would, and wash His hands of us and say, "I am done." But our God isn't like that, He loves, searches and holds us dear while we are making our mess. Then, when we come to our senses He is waiting with open arms to embrace us!

Matthew 6:33 says, *"Seek ye first the kingdom and his righteousness and all these things will be given to you as well."* This verse references how people worry about food, drink, and the clothes that we wear. When I was amidst my mess, most days all I cared about was my next hit. I was homeless, hungry and alone but all I cared about was the needle in my arm. Now I understand that my God was there with me. At the time, you could have told me that, and I would have thought you were nuts. But even then, all these promises were true, I just had my focus wrong. Once we change what we seek, from the sinful habits to the love of Jesus, immediately He is there to accept us and give us what we need. Jesus has offered us what we needed all along but we were to disillusioned to see it and more importantly accept it.

God is not afraid of the messy. That is His specialty. Lepers were among the messiest in Jesus's time. Sent away from their families to live in isolation. Made to ring a bell if they came near others to announce their presence so people could avoid them. Did this deter Jesus? In *Mark 1:40-42* Jesus heals one of these cast out souls. Jesus *"reached out his hand and touched the man."* Don't miss the significance in this. He TOUCHED the filthiest. Jesus could have spoken and the leper would have been healed, but He chose to TOUCH him. He went towards the mess, and showed love. He does that for each of us. Whether He met you in solitary confinement like me or in the shadows of an alley, Jesus is there to love us amidst our mess!

B. Not a religion, it is a relationship

As you progress in your spiritual journey, you may have to deal with some baggage and opinions from your past experiences or from that of others'. One of the primary reasons that people turn away from church or Jesus is a bad experience. The world has learned to equate Jesus with church. The problem with this, is that church is made up of people and people are imperfect. When people get hurt by people in the church, they take offense, leave the church and tell as many people as they can about their bad experiences. You may be one of those people who have been hurt in the church or by the church.

Here is the good news…. Jesus is not the church or even a religion. Jesus spent thirty-three years on earth and he spent very little time in an actual church building. He went out and met people where they were. For you see, Jesus is all about the relationship and not a religion. Too many religions require memberships, rituals, rules and are often very judgmental. Jesus isn't about any of that. But what about the rules? Yes, God desires that we live according to His Word but once you enter into a true relationship with Him, you will want to please Him. You will not want to give into your sinful desires any longer. And it won't be just because of a list of rules, it will be because of a relationship, a two-way relationship. There is a passage in Ephesians that talks about being made alive in Christ and how we changed from being dead in our sin to alive in Christ. This passage will help to cement how God desires a relationship with you and the changes that result from that relationship.

Read ***Ephesians 2:1-10***. So, you see, when we were without Christ we were dead and pleased the sinful nature and now, you are alive with Christ and are free. Soak that in- being a Christian brings freedom, not chains to rules, rituals and rites. This freedom in you will create a clean spirit and a complete new way of living and thinking!!!! Praise God for that! Please don't miss this. For some that have been raised in the church, it is almost as if they are not free. They are burdened by man-made rules and judgement. God wants us to live in complete freedom. Freedom from sin, freedom from condemnation, freedom from rules. Your love and gratitude for Christ will result in obedience to the point that living according to His word is a delight and a privilege!

Being a Christian, a Christ follower, is just that: a close, deep, intimate, personal 2-way relationship full of love and acceptance. So, you need to let go of any old misperceptions and any old hurts that may have been caused within the walls of a church or the structure of a religion. None of that is Jesus' fault, and by holding on to those hurts, you are held back from going deeper into your relationship with Christ. It is not even about a curriculum, not even my curriculum. Yes, I hope and pray that this material will advance your relationship with Christ, but I would never want you to mistake the curriculum as being more important or give it more value than Jesus and what He has for you. How many of you have experienced a situation where people gave a pastor or a church more value and time than they did to Christ himself? That is what I do **not** want. Your first love should always be to Jesus and He deserves your full devotion.

Another concept that is misunderstood with Christians is the fear of the Lord. Many churches teach us to have "the fear of the Lord". This can tend to separate us from Him by painting an inaccurate picture. Some people grow up actually being afraid of God. They perceive that He is an all-powerful being far away from us. Our fear of the Lord is not meant for us to be afraid, we are to be in awe of Him. The closer we draw near to him, the more we will be awestruck by Him. We don't need to fear God, we need to be stunned by all He is. In fact, the opposite is true. Your fear or respect for Him will continue to draw you closer to Him. He wants nothing more than your deep love, affection and closeness. *James 4:7- 8* says "*Submit yourselves, then, to God. Resist the devil and he will flee from you. Come near to God and he come near to you.*" And *Psalm 111:10* says *"The fear of the Lord is the beginning of wisdom; all who follow his precepts have good understanding. To him belongs eternal praise."* Allow those two truths to penetrate your heart today!

C. No sin too big

I am a poster child for this section. I have the privilege to go into prisons in Florida and Texas and preach to women and men who are just like me. I was a 46-time felon! You name it, I probably did it. I was not only bad, I was mean. In prison I was mean just to be mean. And friend, if God can reach down into solitary confinement and save the likes of this sinner, He can and will do it for you too! I have looked into the eyes of many hopeless people, who think they have committed the ultimate sin, or have sinned one time too many! Nope! Remember my nickname for my ministry? "Me too ministry." You tell me what you are going through or where you have been and most likely I can answer, "Me too!" And my favorite me too story is that God took my sins, forgave them and then forgot them! In an instant. Read *Psalm 103:8-12*. What an amazing God we have! He has removed our sins as far as the east is from the west. Now read *Micah 7:18-19*. He hurls our sins into the depths of the sea. He has already forgiven us before we ask Him to. He loves us that much!

Our humanness creates a need to weigh and compare most everything. Who is more successful, who is prettier, skinnier, kinder, etc. Sin is probably at the top of favorite comparisons in the human race. Well, murder has to be the ultimate sin, right? No wait, it has to be homosexuality! In a lot of churches, divorce is the ultimate wrong. But you see, they are all wrong- at least in the eyes of God. You see, a wrong is a wrong to our God. Murder, lying, gossip, promiscuity, all sins, all wrong, all the same to Him. There is no weight applied one over another. It is us who has assigned a severity scale to the sins of the world not God. What you and I need to remember is sin is a wrong choice and they all bring hurt to our Heavenly Father. He wants us to turn away from all wrongdoing and He will forgive us all the same. So, you may have committed one of the world's "ultimate sins" but God looks the same at someone who tears someone apart with their gossip and judgement.

Read *Galatians 5:19-21*. Take a close look there. Sexual sins and jealousy are on the same list. Orgies are right next to jealousy. Yes, being slanderous is a sin and is on the same list as idolatry. In God's eyes, a sin is a sin. What is most important is that you stop sinning, ask for forgiveness and move on. He wants to renew you and then use you for his glory! Say that again, "Renew me and use me." Look at this list of people in the Bible who God chose to use after they made very bad choices:
- Moses, a murderer, led God's people out of Egypt.
- Rehab, a prostitute, rescued spies from death.
- David, and adulterer and murderer was a King and servant of God.
- Paul, persecuted Christians and went on to preach for Christ and wrote most of the New Testament.

There are so many stories of redemption all through scripture. God's design is for us to be free! Free of the burden of sin. Yes, we all have a sinful nature and as long as we walk on this earth we will struggle against it. But, the lesson I hope you have attained in this section is that there is no sin too big for God to redeem and restore! Also, remember that Christ was crucified for all of mine and your sins. He suffered so that we do not have to. Walk in your freedom today!

D. Who or what owns your heart?

This is a very important question and one that you will have to revisit on a regular basis through the remainder of your journey on earth. You see our loyalties are so important and when we give them to other areas, it leaves less and less time for your relationship with Christ. This is not to say that you have to do nothing but read the Bible, what I am addressing is giving your affection to other areas. This can be unhealthy relationships, addictions, success in your career and even material items. Read the following verses:
- *Psalms 62:10*
- *Romans 12:2*
- *Jeremiah 29:13*
- *Matthew 22:37*

God doesn't want just a piece of your heart, He wants your entire devotion, your first priority. Now, yes, we need to love our family, our friends, and what we do but they are never to take priority over Christ. Ask yourself what have you been giving precedence over God? God wants 100% of your heart!

After reading the last paragraph, you may be defeated by guilt. Stop right there. Remember your old habits do not define you any longer. You are not who you used to be! Think I am wrong? Re-Read *2 Corinthians 5:17*! I like to tell people that I have had a blood transfusion! When I accepted Christ, I truly recognized what He had done for me. His blood cleansed me and my sinful nature. I like to think of it in picture form, my blood, along with my bad habits are no longer there. I now have the blood of my savior coursing through my veins! I have had a complete blood transfusion, so He not only owns my heart but His blood pumps through it.

Do not accept the lies of the devil- your old habits do NOT define you any longer. It is so easy to accept these lies because that is what the world tells you and what Satan is whispering in your ear. But don't listen to them. God is in your heart. God owns your heart. God's blood runs through your heart. I like to tell the girls in my houses that we need to follow Christ with "reckless abandon." Say that phrase out loud three times:

- Reckless abandon
- Reckless abandon
- Reckless abandon

Now- what does it mean to you? To me it means that I am following Christ with everything, everyday, in every way, and without worrying about anything else. Why? Because I know where I was, I now know where I am and most importantly, I know who saved me and got me here. I can never repay God for what He did for me, but I can do this. I can give Him my entire heart and live for Him with a passion that He deserves. Are you with me?

Chapter 4

Worksheet 1

~ Love Amidst my Mess ~

Chapter 4 – Worksheet 1
Love Amidst my Mess

Write out **Romans 5:8** here:

_____

_____

_____

_____

_____

Now re-write it by inserting your name in place of the word us or we:

_____

_____

_____

_____

_____

Wow- God sacrificed his Son for us before we ever thought about leaving our sin life behind. Write out what "while we were still sinners" means in your life. What lifestyle choices are you leaving behind and He is forgiving?

_____

_____

_____

_____

_____

_____

_____

_____

_____

Let's go back to the 2 parables that we referenced in this section. One is the parable of the lost lamb found in *Matt. 18:12, Luke 15:1-7* and the other is the parable of the lost coin found in *Luke 15:8-10*. Read them both again.

Now write one out in present day terms but with Jesus looking for you when you were lost. Let your creative writing juices flow.

_____

_____

_____

_____

_____

_____

_____

_____

_____

_____

_____

_____

_____

_____

_____

_____

_____

_____

_____

_____

_____

_____

_____

_____

_____

_____

_____

It took me a while to truly accept that Christ would have died if it were only for me. How about you? Spend some time in prayer and then write a note of thanks to your Savior for pulling you out of your mess!

_____
_____
_____
_____
_____
_____
_____
_____
_____
_____
_____
_____
_____
_____
_____
_____
_____
_____
_____
_____
_____
_____
_____
_____
_____
_____
_____
_____
_____

Chapter 4

Worksheet 2

~ Not a Religion, It's a Relationship ~

Chapter 4 – Worksheet 2
Not a Religion, It's a Relationship

Have you ever experienced "church hurt" personally? If so write about it. _____

_____

_____

_____

How about a "church hurt" that someone you know went through?

_____

_____

_____

_____

Regardless of how many of these we write down, you will find one common thread; the hurt was **from man not God**. Be sure to remember that when dealing with any of these hurts.

What is your church background? Write about it here:

_____

_____

_____

_____

_____

_____

Read *Ephesians 2:1-10* then answer the following questions:

1. How does verse 1 describe us when we were in our sin?

   _____

2. Who does verse 3 say "lived among them at one time?"

   _____

3. If that is true (which it is) who of us have lived in a mess?

   _____

4. In verse 5, how does it say we are saved?

_____

5. What else does verse 8 say about how we are saved?

_____

_____

_____

_____

6. In verse 9, how are we NOT saved?

_____

7. Because of this, no one should take credit for our salvation. Who is the only one that should take credit?

_____

8. Are you living in this freedom today?

_____

_____

_____

9. If not, what is holding you back?

_____

_____

Let's talk about the fear of the Lord- Have you ever feared God before? Explain?

_____
_____
_____
_____

Do you understand the difference between awe and respect versus true fear?

_____
_____
_____
_____

To help you- think of one thing you have seen in your lifetime that has left you speechless and in complete wonder- what came to mind?

_____

_____

_____

_____

Next- who is the person in your life that you respect the most in this world? _____

_____

_____

_____

_____

Now- I want you to think about your God with total awe and respect. When you fear Him, fear Him with respect for His power, great love and all that He has done for us despite our shortcomings. Talk to Him about all of this.

Chapter 4

Worksheet 3

~ No Sin Too Big ~

Chapter 4 – Worksheet 3
No Sin Too Big

Tell me 3 sins the world think are the greatest sins:

1. _____
2. _____
3. _____

Now, tell me 3 sins that you feel the world think are the least in severity:

1. _____
2. _____
3. _____

- Now, remember what we learned in this lesson. All of these are the same in the eyes of God. So, the person who commits a sin from the second list, are viewed the same as those who commit a sin from the first list.

- And, maybe you committed all of these sins and multiple times- does God's forgiveness cover even that? Read the following verses on forgiveness and write your thoughts beside each:

1. *Psalm 103:3-4*

   _____
   _____

2. *1 John 1:9*

   _____
   _____

3. *Matthew 26:28*

   _____
   _____

4. *Colossians 1:13-14*

   _____
   _____

5. *Ephesians 1:7*

_____

_____

Read *Lamentations 3:55-60*. As you read it, compare it to when you were at your lowest and Christ rescued you. Write your comparisons here:

_____
_____
_____
_____
_____
_____
_____
_____
_____
_____
_____
_____
_____
_____

Give thanks today that our God is a god of grace, mercy, love, forgiveness and redemption. Write a prayer of thanks to your God-

_____
_____
_____
_____
_____
_____
_____
_____
_____
_____
_____
_____
_____
_____

Chapter 4

Worksheet 4

~ Who or What Owns Your Heart? ~

Chapter 4 – Worksheet 4
Who or What Owns your Heart?

Define the following words/phrases in your own words:

Passion-

_____
_____
_____
_____
_____

Pursue-

_____
_____
_____
_____

Reckless Abandon –

_____
_____
_____
_____

Complete Devotion-

_____
_____
_____
_____

Intimacy-

_____
_____
_____
_____

Now- commit to making these statements a regular part of your relationship with Christ. Make Him your number one in all areas of your life. Pray about areas that need to change to make this happen. Below list the areas of your life that take time and devotion and prioritize them with God being in the number one spot.

1. God

2. _____

3. _____

4. _____

5. _____

6. _____

7. _____

8. _____

9. _____

10. _____

RRM Snapshot .... Meet Melanie ~

From what I remember, beginning at the age of four, I was being sold and trafficked without my family knowing. My dad was a drug addict and my mom wasn't around much. I remember needles being stuck in my feet and always feeling dizzy. I never felt alive. My life was completely hidden behind closed doors.

My parents divorced and I would be shuffled back and forth. My dad was homeless, and lived in his car. My mom lived with my grandma. So, I lived in both worlds; having nothing and having everything. When my mother, brother and I moved into an apartment, I began to try drugs on my own. I fell in love with a guy who was a member of the gang, "The Bloods." Living a street life was not for me, but captivity to drugs and him made me a slave and hopeless.

My first suicide attempt was an overdose leaving me breathless in a hospital bed. When I woke up and realized I didn't die, I began to cut my arms. It was an attempt to cover up my unbearable emotional pain.

At age 15, I moved in with my aunt and uncle. I had nightmares and would wet the bed. I felt worthless, dirty, and covered in a darkness. I was admitted into several behavioral centers around Florida, given multiple diagnoses and prescribed different medications. Because of my mental status, my aunt and uncle lost custody of me and I was placed in foster care.

I was officially an orphan. That was a new kind of low and I was placed in a shelter. What seemed bad, turned good and a lady started to take me to church. That is where I met Pastor Dawn and was accepted into her women's home.

In that program, God delivered me from the pits of hell and placed me under His wings where I continue to dwell in his presence today. While at Radical Restoration, I found true freedom from my past and chains. I completed an advanced degree in Bible College. After that, I went on to more classes at Daytona State University and eventually went on to Christ for the Nations where I graduated in 3 years. I have found the love of my life, married him and we are now expecting our first child, a baby boy! I was truly dead but I am now alive and God will always get the glory from my past, present and future.

Chapter 5

Worship

~ Beyond Church Walls ~
~ Daily, Through our Actions ~
~ Leaving Old Idols Behind ~
~ Soaking ~

Chapter 5- Worship

Worship is so much more than what most people know. When you ask someone on the street what worship is, you may get answers like: an idol, singing in church or adoring something or someone. Worship can mean many different things to different people depending on personal backgrounds and environments. In this section, I want to teach you what I have learned about worship and what it means to me.

A. Beyond church walls

First and foremost, worship does not just happen within the walls of a church building!!! It is not only done amidst a large group of other believers. You do not need a praise band, praise team or worship leader to experience worship. You do not need to be led in worship and you do not have to worship a certain way because others around you are acting a certain way. No, worship is not just corporate. Now, don't get me wrong, I love going to church and joining in corporate worship with other believers. I enjoy an amazing worship night where hundreds of voices lift the name of Jesus to the rafters. Being in a Christian concert where thousands of voices join together, lit cell phones swaying back and forth, can feel like heaven has come to earth. Yes, there is a place for corporate worship but I want us to think beyond the walls because some of my own best worship comes in quiet and personal times with God.

The act of worship starts with us acknowledging who Christ is. That can come through simple prayer. When we pray, we acknowledge His existence. Then when we talk to Him, we honor Him. He loves to hear us talk to Him, cry with Him, laugh in His spirit, and sing to Him. Our quiet time is an amazing time to worship our God. Sometimes, I believe that many who have grown up in church miss out on this part of worship because they have unintentionally been trained to believe that worship is only singing in church.

Child of God, take time daily with your God. Talk to Him, openly and candidly about your life. Thank Him for who He is and what He has done in your life and in the lives of those you associate with. Adore His qualities out loud. Confess any wrongdoing in your walk with Him. Lastly, ask Him to help you as you maneuver through this journey. Look up these verses on worship and apply them to your personal time with God:

> *- Psalms 100:2*
> *- Psalms 95:6*
> *- Psalms 63:4*
> *- Psalms 51:15*

We can also worship God through our joy! Joy is not happiness. Joy is a deeper, constant state that is present through a relationship with Christ. Joy perseveres through trials because of the constant state of our God. There is no greater compliment to a Christ follower than when someone comes up to you and says, "There is something different about you. What is it? I want to have what you have." This is the joy of the Lord bubbling out of you, and it is real and cannot be contained. We worship God by sharing with others through our joyful expressions, our acts of kindness and service and of course our words of testimony. What better way to worship God than to share his love with people who do not know Him and to expand His kingdom by doing so! *Psalm 51:12* says *"Restore to me the joy of my salvation and grant me a willing spirit, to sustain me."* This assures us that when we accept Christ, we receive this joy. Then as we walk with Him, experience His freedom, it is so natural to be filled with joy that we have to share it. Look up the following verses about sharing with others with joy:

> *- Psalms 100:1*
> *- Isaiah 24:14*
> *- Psalms 126:3*

One of my friends likes to put it this way, "Splash somebody with the love of Jesus today!" If we can be an extension of Jesus' love, what a better way to worship Him?

B. Daily, through our actions

Every new day creates new worship opportunities. And the excuse, "I am too busy" is not going to fly! Worship is mobile, flexible, and can become almost constant. I love to worship as I drive. Yes, I usually have my God tunes on, but that is not what I am talking about. I am looking for Christ in all things. There is beauty in a cloud formation, trees with fall foliage, fresh fallen snow, birds soaring above me, the sun dancing off a body of water, and the power of a storm. Any of these and more can take me right into a conversation of adoration with God. He is so creative and He didn't have to make the items around us so beautiful.

Our interactions with others is a way to worship Christ too. We first need to think of ourselves as less, and others as more. A good dose of humility goes a long way. We live in a scary and untrusting world. Take time to look people in the eyes. Offer a smile. You may be surprised the reactions that you get. We first need to make time for people. Take time to notice those around you. Do you need to give that elderly shopper a hand with their groceries? How about an encouraging word to a young mother struggling with her charges? Or offering food and a prayer to a homeless and hungry soul? Worship is a verb not a noun. We get that wrong quite a bit. If you say that you haven't had any opportunities to do ministry lately then you are walking with your eyes closed. There are so many needs all around us, we need to worship God by being His hands and feet every day.

We can worship God with our words. Now, the opposite of that is true too, we can dishonor God with our words. A good rule is to **"Pray before you say!"** Take a moment and pray and think about what is about to leave your lips. Once the words are out, they cannot be taken back. A Christian witness can be easily torn down with unkind, harsh and angry words. We need to speak positive words over ourselves and over others. Here are three scriptures that bring truth to this topic:
- ***Proverbs 11:12*** *"Whoever derides their neighbor has no sense, but the one who has understanding, holds their tongue."*

- *Proverbs 12:18* *"The words of the reckless pierce like swords, but the tongue of the wise brings healing."*
- *Proverbs 12:19* *"Truthful lips endure forever, but a lying tongue lasts only a moment."*

Speaking with understanding, wisdom and truth are all ways that we can worship our Lord. I have been told that the mouth is a reflection of the soul and I believe that is so true. What is your mouth telling those around you every day? Now, I know that none of us are perfect. We will all have bad days, but these are goals. Ways that we can strive to best represent Christ. And on days, when you are feeling down? Those are the best days to worship your God!

Staying positive is another act of worship. It is easy to get down when life hands you trial after trial. But, I believe that there are always blessings to be counted. We have a God who loves us. Who died for us so we can have eternal life. He takes care of our every need. Yes, life can be hard but keep your perspective. A good rule is, there is always someone else out there that is worse off than me.

My friend was hospitalized for nine weeks with transverse myelitis when she was only thirty-two. Her three children were young and she was fighting for her life for the 1st two-three weeks of the illness. For the remainder of her hospital stay she fought to learn to walk again. The rest of her hospitalization lasted nine weeks. When I asked her about those times and how she kept her spirits up, her response was, "there was always someone worse off than me in there. I would pray for them and thank God that He was with me." A positive perspective tells others that we serve an amazing God and regardless of the storms of this world, we always have something to praise Him for!!!

C. Leaving old idols behind

Another form of worship is walking in our freedom. If we are to be completely free we need to leave our old idols behind. The Bible is clear that we cannot serve two masters. (*Matthew 6:24 & Luke 16:13*) We have addressed this before but not as a form of worship. If we are still honoring old relationships, practicing old habits and focusing on unhealthy thinking then we are not honoring our God. An idol is anything we hold dear. Addictions are real and hard to break out of without the help of Jesus. And let's be honest, even with Jesus, Satan can whisper lies into our ear that makes it "acceptable" to keep the door open for our bad habits. We need to shut and lock the door on all of our old habits.

To leave our old idols behind, we need to ask ourselves "What did I use to worship before my salvation?" This process takes prayer, transparency and a lot of humility. David's writings in Psalms is a great place to go for an example of both confession and praise. David was broken by his behavior and yearned to be made right in the eyes of God. Let's read part of his writing in *Psalms 139:23-24* "*Search me God, and know my heart; test me and know my anxious thoughts. See if there is any offensive way in me, and lead me in the way everlasting.*"

David's example needs to be a daily ritual for us in our quiet time. We need to actively keep our old ways behind us and our God before us. Our focus needs to be on Christ- not on our old relationships, drug use, mistakes and law breaking behavior. Remember, Christ has forgiven you, now forgive yourself and move on. David again says it best in *Psalms 25:15* "*My eyes are ever on the Lord, for only he will release my feet from the snare.*"

Your thought process is key to who or what your idol is. Here are two phrases that I have challenged others with for years:
1. **You become what you desire.**
2. **You are what you believe.**

What do you desire? What is the first thing that you think about when you wake up in the morning? When the going gets tough, what or who do you turn to? If these answers are not your Jesus, then you may have another idol that needs to be eliminated.

Then, what do you truly believe? Do you fully embrace that God is enough for you? If everything else in your life is stripped away, will He be enough for you? You see, I understand the burning desire for the next hit. I have experienced the need to be "loved" and "needed" by my sugar daddy. I have felt the acceptance of a common goal of people even if those people were my fellow strippers or homeless crew. Familiarity can become an idol. But once you allow God to truly be your focus the rest will fade away. For a moment, I want you to focus on this passage:

II Corinthians 10:3-5 *"For though we walk in the flesh, we are not waging war according to the flesh. For the weapons of our warfare are not of the flesh but have divine power to destroy strongholds. We destroy arguments and every lofty opinion raised against the knowledge of God, and take every thought captive to obey Christ, being ready to punish every disobedience, when your obedience is complete." ESV*

Take every thought captive. Wage war against strongholds. Sometimes we need to speak it out- "Satan I am not that person anymore!" "Get behind me Satan, by the blood of Christ I am redeemed and free." We will talk more about spiritual warfare but this is a great place to introduce it. When it comes down to it, you have to ask yourself, what is your idol (s)? And who do you really serve? There is no greater act of worship than making Christ your one and all! Make Him what you desire daily. Do you believe the Word of God to be true? Then worship Him as your only idol!

D. Soaking

If you have been a part of our ministry or spent any time in one of our houses, you know what soaking is, but let me explain. Soaking is setting aside uninterrupted time to be quiet before the Lord, play worship music, quiet yourself and listen for the voice of God. Our living room regularly is covered with blankets, women laying on their face or kneeling with hands open, our God music playing loudly. During this time, our goals are to:
- Ask Him to show us how He sees us
- Allow Him to heal
- Allow Him to redeem
- Allow Him to restore

The world pulls for our time, but we forget that our Father wants that time as well. It is a proven fact that it is hard to hear when we are constantly talking. This is a common problem today. Either our voices or the roar of the world keeps us so absorbed that it is impossible to hear the voice of God. He can reveal so much to us: about ourselves, about others, and prophecies. I have met many people that say "I wish I could hear the voice of God." You can, but you need to listen. Truly listen, not just a five-minute prayer after your devotions. Soaking accomplishes this in amazing ways.

Allow Him to heal, redeem and restore by opening your hands and heart for Him to move. The Holy Spirit is so real when we soak that you can literally feel Him. Soaking can result in weeping, holy laughter, and a lot of revelation. There is nothing complicated about worship. It is spending time with God. Uninterrupted and quality time with our Lord.

When is the last time you have gotten in tune with His presence? Or even felt his presence? One of the greatest tragedies in the Christian walk is that Christians love God, follow God but don't really spend time with Him, in His presence. An easy analogy is a simple friendship. If you want to be close with a friend, what is the best way to do that? Simple, spend time with them. I am not sure why we expect a closeness with God when we only give Him an hour every Sunday. Once we start to experience the sweetness of our Lord, we will naturally want more.

- *1 Chronicles 16:11* and *Psalms 105:4* "*Seek the Lord and his strength; seek his presence continually.*"
- *Psalms 95:2* "*Let us come into his presence with thanksgiving; let us make a joyful noise to him with songs of praise.*"
- *Psalms 100:2* "*Serve the Lord with gladness! Come into his presence with singing.*"

What you need to remember is this, **in the presence of God- true change comes.** When we make God our only expectation, it is amazing the transformations that occur! Let's read a scripture that will cement this concept"

- *Psalm 62:5-7* "*For God alone, O my soul, wait in silence, for my hope is in him. He only is my rock and my salvation, my fortress; I shall not be shaken. On God rests my salvation and my glory; my mighty rock, my refuge is God.*"
-

Soaking can bring amazing change. Soaking can be done alone or as a group. Regardless of how or when you do it, be assured that God will be there if you invite Him in! A huge part of worship is soaking. Intimacy with God is no sweeter than in some undivided time with your God. You will feel His presence, His love and His embrace. Don't believe me, then try it. Make soaking a regular part of your quiet time! Start today!

Chapter 5

Worksheet 1

~ Beyond Church Walls ~

Chapter 5 – Worksheet 1
Beyond Church Walls

What does worship mean to you?

_____

_____

_____

_____

As mentioned in the lesson, David and the Psalms are great
examples of worship. Here are some additional verses on worship
from Psalms. Look them up and write what they tell you about
worship:

1. **Psalm 100:4**

_____

_____

2. **Psalm 150:2**

_____

_____

3. **Psalm 145:2**

_____

_____

4. **Psalm 105:1**

_____

_____

5. **Psalm 19:1**

_____

_____

Now- Let's look beyond the Psalms for some verses on worship.

1. **John 4:24**

_____

_____

2. **Luke 4:8**

_____

_____

3. *Hebrews 13:15*

_____

_____

4. *Hebrews 12:28*

_____

_____

5. *1 Chronicles 16:8*

_____

_____

In this section, we talked about how our joy can be worship to our God. Have you experienced a time when you weren't happy but still had joy? Explain- _____

_____

_____

_____

Joy is possible even in the dark times when we have Jesus. In fact, the Bible says we are to be joyful in our affliction. Read the following verses and write what they teach you about joy.

1. *James 1:2*

_____

_____

2. *John 15:11*

_____

_____

3. *1 Peter 1:8,9*

_____

_____

_____

4. *1 Thessalonians 5:16*

_____

_____

5. *Acts 13:32*

_____

_____

This chapter is all about worship- close this worship with a time of prayer and worship. Quiet yourself before God, turn on some music and write any thoughts here:

_____

_____

_____

_____

_____

_____

_____

_____

_____

_____

_____

_____

_____

_____

_____

_____

_____

_____

_____

_____

_____

_____

_____

_____

_____

_____

_____

_____

_____

Chapter 5

Worksheet 2

~ Worship Daily, Through our Actions~

Chapter 5 – Worksheet 2
Daily, Through our Actions

God's creation is a perfect catapult into worship with our God. List ten items from the world God created that draws you into a worshipful and thankful state.

1. _____ 2. _____
3. _____ 4. _____
5. _____ 6. _____
7. _____ 8. _____
9. _____ 10. _____

We can worship God through our interactions with others. God wants us to love one another and respect one another. Sometimes we can be Jesus through a look, smile or act. Write 3 examples of when someone was Jesus to you:

1. _____
_____

2. _____
_____

3. _____
_____

Now, write 3 times of when you were Jesus to someone else:

1. _____
_____

2. _____
_____

3. _____
_____

Our words can be for good or for bad. Read the following verses on the power of our words:

1. *1 Thessalonians 5:11*

   _____

   _____

2. *Ephesians 4:29-32*

   _____

   _____

   _____

   _____

   _____

The old adage "sticks and stones can break my bones but words can never hurt me" has been around a long time. It holds no truth. Often words carry more weight than physical injuries. Take some time to confess words that you have spoken to and about others. Make a commitment here to worship Christ with your mouth.

_____

_____

_____

_____

_____

_____

_____

_____

_____

_____

_____

Chapter 5

Worksheet 3

~ Leaving Old Idols Behind ~

Chapter 5 – Worksheet 3
Leaving Old Idols Behind

Ok, time for more transparency – if you haven't noticed, this is and will continue to be a common thread in this curriculum. Get ready to be open and honest to God and to those around you as a lifestyle change.

So, what are some idols that you use to serve:

1. _____
2. _____
3. _____
4. _____
5. _____
6. _____
7. _____
8. _____
9. _____
10. _____

Now, prayerfully do some self-examination and ask yourself if have allowed any of those to remain open, even if it is even a crack. Be honest with yourself and with your God. He knows it anyway.

_____
_____
_____
_____
_____
_____
_____
_____
_____
_____
_____
_____
_____

Now, let's turn it to the positive. Let's talk about how God is going to be your only idol. How are you going to commit to worship, prayer and Bible time? Make a plan and then share it with someone you can trust and pray about it together.

_____

_____

_____

_____

_____

_____

_____

_____

_____

_____

_____

_____

_____

_____

_____

_____

_____

_____

_____

_____

_____

_____

_____

_____

_____

_____

_____

_____

_____

_____

Chapter 5

Worksheet 4

~ Soaking ~

Chapter 5 – Worksheet 4
Soaking

This worksheet is going to be an activity. There is no better way to teach soaking than to have you actually do it. For this exercise, you need to plan two separate times to soak. What does this require? Set aside one full hour for each soaking. Plan a time with no interruptions, dim the lights, get your favorite Christian music playlist going, make yourself comfortable (you can kneel, sit, lay down), and allow time just for you and God to commune. On this sheet, I want you to write what God revealed, taught or showed you while you soaked, and then of course share it with someone! God is so good, go fellowship with Him!

Response from Soaking #1-

_____

_____

_____

_____

_____

_____

_____

_____

_____

_____

_____

_____

_____

_____

_____

_____

_____

_____

_____

_____

_____

_____

_____

Response from Soaking #2-

RRM Snapshot .... Meet Belinda

As a small child, I struggled with not being enough and feelings of emptiness consumed me to the point of several suicide attempts. By the age of 12 I was using multiple types of drugs. From the ages of 14-16, I was running the streets and ended up abused repeatedly. Through my childhood, I was confined in foster homes, juvenile detention centers, girls' programs and mental health institutions.

By the age of 16, I ended up in prison as a youth offender. At age 21, I was serving my third prison sentence. Even in prison, I continued to make poor choices and used drugs. Eventually, I was sent to solitary confinement. I sat locked in a cell abandoned, hopeless and addicted. I realized that I had spent over half my life in some kind of institution.

Sitting alone in that cell I was uneducated, crippled by fear and desperate for a new life. Through all of that I heard God whisper, "I love you Belinda." These are words I had never heard before and they shook me to the core. Then God said, "Belinda, will you give me your life?" I began to weep. I was overwhelmed by love and peace. I began to tell him, "Yes, Yes, Yes, I will give you my life."

I have never looked back. I quit the drugs, smoking, and even my psychotropic drugs from that day forward. I was completely set free! I spent my days choosing to love and forgive God, myself, and those who had hurt me. I felt God urge me to ask the officer for a Bible. They gave me one but I only had a first-grade education so could only read the easy words. God was faithful. He taught me a word at a time. Once released from solitary, I signed up for educational classes. After one year of very hard work, I graduated with my high school diploma.

Once released from prison, I was accepted into Radical Restoration Ministry home and went through the program that taught me so much more about God and myself. When Dawn shared her story and struggle it gave me hope that I could do it too. Part of the program while at the home included a full scholarship to Bible college and in 2018, I graduated with a Master's degree in theology. I went from being illiterate to having a postgraduate degree!!!

I had not dreamed in years but I began to dream the last year in prison and I saw pictures of children starving physically and spiritually all over the world. I knew that God was calling me to do mission work. After graduating from Radical Restoration, I was able to go to Africa and work with the orphans that I had seen in my dreams. I have held jobs including housekeeper, care taker, equine therapist and even a school teacher.

The last seven years of my life have been beautiful and terrifying at the same time. I have faced old fears and new ones daily. My Lord guides me continually. Every year is filled with love, unfolding and flourishing like a beautiful flower. Relationships being restored and new ones created! His love is freedom and is chasing us all down. Across the room, or across the world, I will follow Jesus anywhere!

Chapter 6

Inner Healing

~ Generational Curses ~

~ Counterfeits ~

~ Deliverance from Strongholds
& Oppression ~

~ Healing the Soul ~

Chapter 6- Inner Healing

This chapter is very important to your journey. We will be looking at some deep-seeded issues that may have been buried for a very long time, but need to be addressed so you can be all you can be for Christ. I have had to go through this process myself, and although it can be hard to face, being on the other side you will find it well worth your time and transparency. So, let's prepare to be honest (once again), and kick some strongholds out of our life!

A. Generational curses

This phrase is just what you think. Something that is passed down from generation to generation and is a curse. The definition of a curse is "a prayer or invocation for harm or injury to come upon one" or "evil or misfortune that comes as if in response or retribution." So, basically what we are talking about are negative behaviors, sins, emotions or habits that are passed down from generation to generation and result in harm, in this case spiritually. Our goal in this chapter is to change the trajectory of any of these curses in your life. One example is sexual abuse. If there has been sexual abuse in one generation, the chance of that continuing to another is very high unless the chain is broken. There are many examples of generational curses, some are obvious, others may not be. Here are some examples:
- Pride
- Poverty
- Fear/ anxiety
- Sexual promiscuity
- Addictions
- Manipulation
- Shame
- Anger
- Rebellion

Now, this list is not all of them by any means. There could be many more, go back to the definition above and some soul searching will do the rest.

So, how do I break the chain you ask?

Here are a few steps to your freedom: *Do not actually do these steps yet- wait for the worksheet.*
1. **Search your heart**- write down any sins or behaviors of yourself or from any of your family members that have affected you. Nothing is too big or too small. Be honest and brainstorm. Recall from when you were very little to present day.
2. **Forgive** – Yourself and anyone else involved.
3. **Pray-** For God to break the cycle.
4. **Rebuke-** Satan and his desire for you to keep this curse active.

We will go into more details on the worksheet for this section.

Generational curses are nothing new. They have been around since biblical times. Let's take a look at some scriptures and see what they tell us:
- *Leviticus 21:39- 42 "And those of you who are left shall rot away in your enemies' lands because of their iniquity, and also because of the iniquities of their fathers they shall rot away like them. But if they confess their iniquity and the iniquity of their fathers in their treachery that they committed against me, and also in walking in contrary to me, so that I walked contrary to them and brought them into the land of their enemies- if then their uncircumcised heart is humbled and they make amends for their iniquity, then I will remember my covenant with Jacob, and I will remember my covenant with Isaac and my covenant with Abraham and I will remember the land."*

This scripture will be key in this section. As you read through this it acknowledges the existence of generational sin, the damage it can do but also the promise of forgiveness if we confess the sins that God will remember and restore us!
- *1 Kings 16:13 "for all the sins of Baasha and the sins of Elah his son, which they sinned and which they made Israel to sin, provoking the Lord God of Israel to anger with their idols."*

- *2 Kings 15:9* *"And he did what was evil in the sight of the Lord, as his fathers had done. He did not depart from the sins of Jeroboam the son of Nebat, which he made Israel to sin."*
- *Numbers 14:18* *"The Lord is slow to anger and abounding in steadfast love, forgiving iniquity and transgression, but he will by no means clear the guilty, visiting the iniquity of the fathers on the children, to the third and the fourth generation. Please pardon the iniquity of this people, according to the greatness of your steadfast love, just as you have forgiven this people, from Egypt until now."*

As you can see, generational sin has been with us for a long time. It is a tool of the devil and it IS possible to break out of but there is action that has to be taken before that can happen. Do you want to be free from the sins of past generations? I know I did and I am glad that I went through the process. In my opinion, my sin was heavy enough, I didn't want to carry the sins of others in addition.

Forgiving generational transgressions also brings understanding of your own sin. As I went through the process, I was amazed how much I understood about myself. Here are some examples: a victim became victimized because of the sexual abuse from her father; a person with a negative spirit recognizes that she listened to her mother's negative words her entire life; a judgmental person now sees the judgmental tone from a grandfather. Now, don't get me wrong, we still need to take responsibility for our wrongs but this process may bring better understanding to your sin life. In the worksheet for this lesson, I will walk you through the actual act of releasing the sins of your past generations. Get ready to be free!

B. Counterfeits

One discovery that I have made through my healing process is the existence of counterfeits the world offers in attempt to replace the genuine item in the spiritual realm. If you haven't figured it out yet, Satan is cunning and fights hard to keep you under his control. Let's read a couple verses on this fallen angel.

1 Peter 5:8 *"Be sober, be watchful; your adversary the devil, as a roaring lion, walks about seeking who he may devour."*
Ephesians 6:11 *"Put on the whole armor of God, that ye may be able to stand against the schemes of the devil."*

When you accepted Christ, you belong to him and Satan no longer has a hold on you. But… he will still try to throw you off, discourage you and lead you astray. The counterfeits that Satan offers, many in the world accept to be as good as what Christ offers. I did for a long time. I did not even realize that I was walking an evil lifestyle because it all seemed so normal. Here are a few of the counterfeits that I have lived:

Counterfeit from Satan	Genuine from Christ
Promiscuous lifestyle	Passion for Christ
Sex/Lust	Intimacy with Christ
Gluttony	Being filled with the Holy Spirit
Needle in the arm	Jesus' blood in my veins
Addictions	Devotion to Christ
Love of Money	Eternal blessings

Satan will try to entice you with just about anything, and tell you that what he offers is better. The truth of the matter is, his road leads to death and life with Christ leads to life. His world is full of darkness, and God's is full of light. Satan does not know how to love, he only knows control. Satan's ways are chaotic and God's are peaceful. Do you see the trend here?

Here are a few keys to overcoming counterfeits in your life:

1. **Know your enemy**- I have written a few facts here but it is important to not underestimate Satan's power and pull. Now granted, Christ is and always be more powerful, but Satan will try to cause you to forget or doubt that.
2. **Recognize and name your counterfeits**- Once you actually claim what you have wrongly given devotion to, you can avoid ever accepting that counterfeit again.
3. **Ask God for forgiveness**- God is working on you. Asking God to clean you of these counterfeits is so very important in your healing. He wants your complete devotion and this step is imperative for that.
4. **Seek wisdom**- We will talk more about this step in chapters seven and eight, and how to walk out some of these areas practically. But going to God's word is always my first stop. Proverbs is the book of wisdom. There are thirty-one chapters and I encourage people I minister to, to read a chapter every day of the month. So, on the 1st, you will read chapter one, on the 15th you will read chapter fifteen, etc. God wants to bestow wisdom on you and knowing how to discern good from evil is a huge part of that wisdom.

Satan is the father of lies- Christ is truth

John 8:44 *"You belong to your father, the devil and you want to carry out your father's desire. He was a murderer from the beginning, not holding to the truth for there is no truth in him. When he lies, he speaks his native language for he is a liar and the father of lies."*

John 14:6 *"Jesus answered, I am the way, the truth, and the life. No one comes to the Father except through me."*

Counterfeits are real. They can be very enticing. But there is nothing better than what God intends and plans for your life. Which father will you serve? Keep your eyes on God and He will guide, sustain and prosper you better than anything that the world has to offer!

C. Deliverance from Strongholds & Oppression

Let's start with strongholds. What are they? A stronghold is just like is sounds, something or someone that has a mighty clamp on your life. Most people think of addictions as the only stronghold but these unhealthy chains can be relationships, habits, gambling, foul language, pride, anger, fear, deception and even control. You may have been held by some of these in the past or maybe still are being grasped by some today. Can I ask you a couple questions?

1. What is the first thing you think of when you wake up in the morning?
2. What are you focusing on when you fall asleep at night?
3. What do you turn to when you are stressed or have a bad day?
4. Has your mind went to any of these (or others) in the last month?
5. How do you spend your money and your time?
6. Is there a habit, behavior or relationship that you have quit and then returned to once or more than once?

If you answered any of these questions with something that is not God honoring then you have a stronghold in your life. We have already spoke about Satan in this chapter and strongholds are another way of him keeping his claws in you. He also delights in secrecy and keeping these habits in the dark. Admitting and dealing with strongholds brings them to the light and they lose their power. But, like counterfeits, you have to slam the door, and lock the lock, deadbolt and safety chain! Then you turn and run the complete opposite direction and don't look back. One of my favorite phrases is "don't pet a demon!" You have to want it gone and you have to be intentional to cast it out.

Oppression is strongly linked and often the cause of strongholds. Oppression is caused by demonic control in your life. Yes, demons are real. Yes, they are Satan's worker bees, and yes, they are out to destroy what they can. Let's read some scripture:

- ***Ephesians 6:12***: *"For our wrestling is not against flesh and blood, but against the principalities, against the powers, against the world rulers of this darkness, against the spiritual hosts of wickedness in the heavenly places.*
- ***Revelation 16:14*** *"for they are spirits of demons, working signs; which go forth unto the kings of the whole world, to gather them together unto the war of the great day of God, the Almighty."*
- ***1 John 3:8*** *"he that doeth sin is of the devil; for the devil sinneth from the beginning. To this end was the Son of God manifested, that he might destroy the works of the devil."*

I have had demons and now I am what my friends call a "professional demon buster." It's true. Spiritual warfare is real and when you receive the Holy Spirit, you also receive power over demons and with the power of Christ within you, you can cast out these stronghold-making, oppression-clutching demons. Now, don't get me wrong, it is a true fight. These armies of Satan do not like to let go. I have experienced being with another prayer warrior, praying in the Spirit over and with individuals to free them from their oppressions, and it can be true warfare. There are a few things that need to happen. The oppressed person has to want them to leave, the people praying have to be bold and be armed with scripture, and the name of Jesus has to be spoken loudly. There is nothing demons hate more than the name of Jesus.

A demon or unclean spirit are controlling and manipulative. A stronghold of fear can be from demons of worry, anxiety, or dread. A stronghold of sexual sins may be from demons of lust, perversion, or abuse. A stronghold of unforgiveness may be a result of judgement, bitterness or revenge. Are you starting to see how they are connected and even intertwined? When someone talks about being in chains spiritually, this is what they are referring to. Strongholds and oppression can literally bind you and keep you completely ineffective and away from a relationship with Christ. But, the great news is that we do not have to stay bound. Christ is and always will promise freedom!

- ***John 8:36*** *"If the Son sets you free, you are free indeed."*
- ***Galatians 5:1*** *"For freedom did Christ set us free: stand fast therefore, and be not entangled again in a yoke of bondage."*
- ***2 Corinthians 3:17*** *"Now the Lord is the Spirit: and where the Spirit of the Lord is, there is liberty."*

D. Healing the Soul

Our souls are uniquely designed to belong to God. With all the muddiness of generational sin, counterfeits and strongholds, our souls are often surrendered to acts and people that they should not be. This sharing of our souls develops unhealthy relationships that in turn create soul ties. Once a soul tie is produced, it holds the person tightly and inhibits and sometimes halts the spiritual relationship that person is intended to have with Christ and also with their intended mate. Take a minute and re-read that paragraph, it is so important.

The following scriptures talk about the soul. Read and absorb their truths:

Psalm 42:1-2 *"As the deer pants for the streams of water, so my **soul** pants for you O, God. My **soul** thirsts for God, for the living God. When can I go, and meet with God?"*

Psalm 42:5 *"Why are you so downcast oh my **soul**? Why so disturbed within me? Put your hope in God, for I will yet praise him, my savior and my God."*

Psalm 62:5 *"Find rest, O, my **soul**, in God alone. My hope comes from him. He alone is my rock and my salvation; he is my fortress. I will not be shaken."*

Proverbs 13:3 *"He who guards his lips guards his **soul**, but he who speaks rashly will come to ruin."*

Proverbs 22:5 *"In the paths of the wicked lie thorns and snares, but he who guards his **soul** stays far from them."*

Matthew 11:29-30 *"Take my yoke upon you and learn from me for I am gentle and humble in heart and you will find rest for your **souls**. For my yoke is easy and my burden is light."*

Matthew 22:37-38 *"Jesus replied, Love the Lord your God with all your heart and with all your **soul** and with all your might. This is the first and greatest commandment."*

Walking in true freedom requires that your soul is connected to God first. Healing the soul means being completely transparent with any indiscretions that have taken place. "But haven't we already done this?", you may ask. This is a deeper connection and confession than any of the others. A soul tie is a deep bond with a habit, a lifestyle, an addiction that needs to be given back to the correct master, Jesus Christ.

The next step to complete freedom is making sure that your physical soul tie is given only to the mate that God intended for you. Scripture is very clear about sexual sins. A sexual sin bears a different weight and therefore a different repercussion. Read this:

1 Corinthians 6:18-20 *"Flee from sexual immorality. All other sins a man commits are outside of his body, but he who sins sexually, sins against his own body. Do you not know that your body is a temple of the Holy Spirit, who is in you, whom you have received from God? You are not your own; you were bought with a price. Therefore, honor God with your body."*

When you give your body to someone else, there is an intimacy there that creates a bond. That bond can be healthy and prosperous if in the boundaries of marriage or it can be destructive and deadly if done any other way. Look back up at the scriptures from Psalms. David wrote those and one of the reasons David was in such turmoil was because he committed adultery with Bathsheba. He knew it was wrong but he did it anyway. He lusted after her with his eyes and then gave into his desires and then his soul was in turmoil. Why? Because he had sinned against his body and against his wife and against his God!

Homosexuality is a sin against your body and your God. Adultery, promiscuous sex with multiple partners are all sins within and against your body. Many people give the excuse, "it was just sex." No. Scripture is clear, we are to honor him with our bodies. These sins produce unhealthy soul ties that unless broken, will continue to haunt you and halt your spiritual growth unless they are dealt with properly! They will also create a wedge between you and your present or future spouse (whichever may be the case). You cannot give your entire self to someone else if part of it still belongs to someone else!

So, with all that said, who does your soul belong to today? Are there soul ties in your life that you have buried and tried to forget? You may think you have buried them and they will never be found out but soul ties WILL resurface and the longer you allow them to exist, the more harm they will cause to you, your family and your relationship with Christ. We need to break them and this is how: Forgiving others who have hurt us, talk out how it affected us, forgiving our self and forgiving Jesus and then seeing Jesus for who He is…. Our Savior and deliverer. He did not cause your circumstances but He is willing and ready to deliver you from them.

The worksheet will provide steps to break your unhealthy soul relationships.

Chapter 6

Worksheet 1

~ Generational Curses ~

Chapter 6 – Worksheet 1
Generational Curses

Ok, here we go. Let's get right to it. Before we start the steps, look up the following scriptures and answer the questions that follow:

Read Ezekiel 18:20-22
1. What do these verses tell us happens if we turn from all our sins?

    _____

2. Will our transgressions be remembered by God?

    _____

3. Are we promised death or life?

    _____

Read I John 2:1-2.
1. Jesus is the _____ for our sins.
2. What does the word propitiation mean? _____

    _____

    _____

3. Whose sins does he cover?

    _____

These scriptures can give us great assurance in the process that we are about to take part in. We are going to go step by step through the process and start-breaking some generational chains! Before beginning be sure to take some time and pray for God's direction, revelation and wisdom in this process.

1. **Search your heart**- write down any sins or behaviors of yourself, or from any of your family members that have affected you. Nothing is too big or too small. Be honest and brainstorm. Recall from when you were very little to present day.
    -   Use a separate piece of paper and literally start writing. Any hurt, sin, words or actions that caused you pain.

Don't overthink this. Just write what comes to your mind: what the sin was, who was involved and when it was.

- Now that you have your list, you will need to do steps 2-4 for every hurt that you wrote down. Remember, nothing is too big or too small.

2. **Forgive** – Yourself and anyone else involved.
3. **Pray-** For God to break the cycle.
4. **Rebuke-** Satan and his desire for you to keep this curse active.

A sample prayer could look something like this:

Dear Father in Heaven-
Thank you for bringing to my healing process the remembrance of the _____(sin) that happened _____ (time) and involved _____ (people/ person). Please forgive me for my part in this sin and forgive _____ (people/ person) for their part. Father I ask that you break the cycle and hold of this sin in my life and in the life of my children and grandchildren and generations to come. I rebuke Satan and the hold this has had on our family. Thank you, God, for your healing power!

Feel free to add to or delete from this prayer. It is important to say these prayers out loud and to claim them boldly! It is very normal to get emotional and you may need to take breaks. It is not uncommon to have quite a list but be sure to pray over each hurt. I find it very helpful to have someone be there with you or for you to share with them after these steps. Accountability is very positive and strengthens the boldness of this faith step. I am so proud of you! You can come back to this anytime if you think of other areas that you failed to address.

Chapter 6

Worksheet 2

~ Counterfeits ~

Lesson 6 – Worksheet 2
Counterfeits

Ok- for the first part of this worksheet I want you to do another brainstorming session. This one is not personal, and should be easier than some of the others we have done. Below I want you to write out as many attributes of God and Satan that you can think of. Go!

Attributes of God	**Attributes of Satan**

Now- I want you to write out what your counterfeit(s) were, and possibly still are and what you feel they were replacing that God had for you instead. This one may take a bit longer. Again, let's take some time in prayer before you start writing.

Counterfeit	God's plan
1. _____	_____
2. _____	_____
3. _____	_____
4. _____	_____
5. _____	_____ \

Use the back or additional paper as needed- be sure to write them all.

Scripture- Go back to the counterfeit lesson and write out your favorite verse from that lesson. Commit it to memory so you can defend yourself from future counterfeits.

_____
_____
_____

Prayer time-
Take some time to talk to God about these counterfeits in your life. How did these falsehoods affect you? Thank Him for His goodness to you. And of course, ask for forgiveness for allowing Satan to mislead you.

Chapter 6

Worksheet 3

~ Deliverance from Strongholds & Oppression ~

Lesson 6 – Worksheet 3
Deliverance from Strongholds & Oppression

1. What strongholds can you identify in your life? List them
   here:

   _____

   _____

   _____

   _____

   _____

   _____

   _____

2. Take a deep look inside of your heart. What of these
   strongholds are still active and are you ready to be free from
   them? Write your response here:

   _____

   _____

   _____

   _____

   _____

   _____

   _____

   _____

   _____

   _____

   _____

3. Look up the following verses and write next to them what
   you learned:
   - *Mark 16:17 -*

   _____

   _____

   _____

- *Luke 10:18-19-*

_____
_____
_____

- *Matthew 10:8 -*

_____
_____
_____

4. Now, for the next part of this exercise you will need to have others with you to pray with and for you. Here are the steps to take if you want to break the chains of your strongholds and oppressions:
   a. Have 1-2 people who are familiar with praying out demons join you.
   b. Review your list of strongholds with them.
   c. Talk through what your desire is.
   d. Pray together in the name of Jesus and with the power of the Holy Spirit to cast out any demons that are holding you captive.
   e. When that step is complete, pray that the Holy Spirit fill you in a new and powerful way.
   f. Take some time to celebrate by soaking and worship your God!

Chapter 6

Worksheet 4
~ Healing the Soul ~

Lesson 6 – Worksheet 4
Healing the Soul

We are going to start this worksheet by answering some questions from the last paragraph from this lesson:

1. Who does your soul belong to today?

   _____

2. Are there soul ties in your life that you have buried and tried to forget? Can you name people you have had affairs with, had homosexual relations with, been promiscuous with? List them here:

   _____
   _____
   _____
   _____
   _____
   _____

3. Is it your desire to have these ties cut once and for all and to give your soul to who it rightly belongs?

   _____
   _____

4. Let's start by looking up the following verses on forgiveness and writing what you learned from them:
   - *Matthew 18:21-22*

   _____

   - *Ephesians 4:32*

   _____

   - *Matthew 6:14- 15*

   _____

   - *Colossians 3:13*

   _____
   _____

5. Forgive others who have hurt you, write about your hurt here and then forgive that person(s).

_____
_____
_____
_____
_____
_____
_____

6. Forgive yourself- this one is hard but necessary. Write out your forgiveness to yourself here.

_____
_____
_____
_____

7. Many people blame Jesus for their past and their hurt. If that is you confess that here. Talk to Jesus about your feelings.

_____
_____
_____
_____
_____

8. If you have a mate that has been affected by your soul tie, you need to make that relationship right. Make a plan here.

_____
_____
_____
_____
_____
_____
_____
_____
_____
_____
_____
_____

Now it is time to truly break these soul ties. So, for each name you wrote under #2, you need to go through the following steps. You have to do each individually. It is recommended to have someone with you as you pray.

1. Confess your sin(s) using the name of the person and specific. Speaking them out brings them to light.
2. Ask God to forgive you.
3. Ask God to break the soul tie.
4. Ask God to remove the importance and memories of this soul tie, so there is no longer an attraction to return.
5. Commit your soul to Christ.

When you have gone through each person. You can repeat these steps for any painful memories that have also created unhealthy soul ties.

Spend time soaking to give God praise for his faithfulness in your freedom and healing!!!! This was hard work and He is worthy of all the praise and Glory!

RRM Snapshot .... Meet Jessica ~

At the age of 12, I began smoking pot to fit in with my older siblings and friends. I had everything a child could ever want growing up from material items to a loving family, still I felt incomplete.

For the next 17 years, I continued to use drugs. I tried to get sober and tried rehab after rehab. None were successful or lasting. To everyone around me, I had a great life and should have been happy, yet I felt so miserable inside. I was angry at myself for not being happy. My addiction began to spiral out of control. I was taking deadly amounts of heroin, Xanax, and pain pills daily. I overdosed three times within a month and a half.

Each time I woke up in a hospital, strapped to a bed, on a respirator, and in intensive care. Each time I was told I should have not survived. The doctors told me and my family that if I continued on that path, I would end up dead. At 29, I began to wonder if God truly had a purpose for my life. Why was I still alive?

It was not even a week later when Pastor Dawn came to Indiana to help open a Dream Center. Out of desperation, ladies from my church set up a meeting with her and I. Moments after meeting with her, I knew I wanted what she had. She asked me if I wanted to go home to Florida with her the next day and I quickly said yes! I flew to Florida with her the next day and found real freedom. I was freed from a 17-year drug addiction. My relationship with my husband and children was restored. I no longer felt lonely, hopeless and empty. God worked a miracle in my life. Dawn and the girls at the house gave me the nickname Lazarus because I have truly been raised to life.

Since my time at Radical Restoration Ministries God has continued to work in my life. He has led me to open a women's home like Dawn's in Indiana. The name of the ministry is the Remnant house and I am so incredibly blessed to share the power of God's freedom with women who are in this ministry. I now know why God kept me alive all those years ago. He saved me so I could share his love with others and save them too!

Chapter 7

Pitiful or Powerful

~ Living the Victorious Life ~
~ Powerful Thoughts ~
~ Powerful Words ~

Chapter 7- Pitiful or Powerful

Congratulations for all the hard work that you have done over the last 6 chapters. My hope is you are enjoying your first steps in real freedom. Now, we need to talk about next steps. How do you keep walking with Christ, continuing your growth and journey the best way possible? Where do I go from here? The next two chapters will address these issues. The Christian life is rewarding but not without pitfalls, so let's get you prepared. Let's be powerful and not pitiful!

A. Living the Victorious Life

Once you are free it is time to leave the role of victim behind. That can be difficult if that is the only role you have played for a very long time. With God's power, you are now victorious not victimized. The Bible is clear that the Christian life brings victory!

- *1 Corinthians 15:57 "But thanks be to God, who gives us the victory through our Lord Jesus Christ."*
- *Deuteronomy 20:4 "...for the Lord your God is he who goes with you to fight for you against your enemies to give you the victory."*
- *1 John 5:4 "For everyone who has been born of God overcomes the world. And this is the victory that has overcome the world—our faith."*
-

Praise God for His victory in your life!

The eagle is mentioned in scripture 26 times. There is a reason, we are to be an eagle in our Christian walk. They are bold, not afraid to fly alone, they fly above the storm, they build their foundation on a firm place and have amazing vision. Now take those qualities and apply them to your Christian walk. We are to be bold. We should be confident enough to stand alone if we have to. Our foundation is solid because it built on Jesus. And our vision will be amazing because God will show you new adventures and dreams as you go.

An eagle will also not cower in a storm, instead they fly above the storm and use the extra wind currents to help them soar higher. Isn't that amazing!!! To live a victorious life, you have to learn to stay true when trials come, and they will come. It is so tempting to go back to old habits or to blame God when something doesn't go as planned but that is our old behavior. We have left that behind. **John 16:33** says *"In this world you WILL have trouble, but take heart, I have overcome the world."* This does not say you **may** have trouble. Because we live in a fallen world, unfortunately there **is** trouble, pain and sorrow. So, how do I stay victorious amidst the storm? Here are a few of my favorite sayings:

- **It's darkest before the storm** – we have all seen a thunderstorm. The clouds roll in, everything gets dark, the winds pick up. Then the storm. But remember, the storm will pass. It is temporary. And what does a storm bring? Rain, renewal for dryness. That is such truth! Often, our storms will bring us much needed renewal when our walk is getting dull.

James 1: 2-6 addresses this: *"Count it all joy, brothers, when you face trials of many kinds, for you know that the testing of your faith produces perseverance and perseverance hope. And let hope have its full effect that you may be perfect and complete, lacking in nothing."*

Well, that says it all- our testing strengthens us. It seasons and perfects us, producing qualities in us that we were lacking in. I know that I am constantly growing. Every new trial brings knowledge, wisdom and stretching. Stretching is not always comfortable, is it? No, but it results in change. So, remember after the storm, the sun comes back out!

- **Laugh out loud in it**- enjoy the journey! Just like *James 1:2* says above, count it joy. Face trials with a smile on your face. Make people around you wonder, "what does she have that I don't?" I guarantee those around me have scratched their heads wondering more than once. I am just oozing with praises and his joy OOZES out of me.

- **If you don't quit you win.** – you have to stay in the race to win. *Philippians 3:14 says "I press on toward the goal to win the prize for which God has called me heavenward in Christ Jesus."* In the Christian walk, it is not what place you finish in, but that you finish, and finish well. The verse says "press on". That requires action. Stay in it, God has something to teach you through the hard times.

- **Breakthrough is on the other side.** - Just as the storm brings renewal, moisture and fresh sunshine, your breakthrough is right around the corner and promises you new growth. So, embrace your difficulties and ask God what He would like you to learn from them. Don't waste a chance to gain a new perspective and please don't give up before your breakthrough comes! *James 1:12 "Blessed is the one who perseveres under trial because, having stood the test, that person will receive the crown of life that the Lord has promised to those who love him."*

I don't know about you but I do not want to miss out on that crown or the eternal life that He has promised us!

B. Powerful Thoughts

The next way to stay powerful and not pitiful is through a healthy thought life. This concept may seem foreign to you but is so essential to overall spiritual health. I don't know about you, but I spend a lot of time in my thoughts. You can call it day dreaming, planning what I need to next, a running list in my head or just vegging, but if your thoughts go the wrong direction, you can become pitiful quickly.

- Our thoughts determine our decisions; our decisions determine our destiny. This teaching holds so much truth and weight. If you spend a lot of time thinking on your past life, you likely will make a decision to go back and then that becomes your destiny.

Example- **Thought-** I want to get high.

Decision- I find my old dealer and make a purchase.

Destiny- I have relapsed and am back in my old life.

But, if your thoughts are on Christ, your decisions will be grounded in love and your destiny will be eternal life with Him.

Example- **Thought-** I need to spend time with Jesus.

Decision- I do my personal devotions and watch a sermon.

Destiny- I have grown in my personal walk and strengthened my faith.

Where does your thought life take you? Which one sounds more like you? You need to do some self-examination if your thought life is weak because your decisions and destiny are right behind.

- Think about what you are thinking about- What are you entertaining in your mind? The mind is a door into the heart and soul. One of my favorite passages is *Philippians 4:8* *"Finally, brothers and sisters, whatever is true, whatever is noble, whatever is right, whatever is pure, whatever is lovely, whatever is admirable—if anything is excellent or praiseworthy—think about such things."*

There is so much to gain from this verse. Read it again. Write it on notecards and put it on your mirror and fridge. Commit it to memory. Some of the work that we did on counterfeits, strongholds, and unhealthy soul beliefs may try to resurface in your thought process regularly. If that happens, give it the "whatever test":

- Whatever is true?
- Whatever is noble?
- Whatever is right?
- Whatever is pure?
- Whatever is lovely?
- Whatever is admirable?
- Whatever is excellent or praiseworthy?

Does the thought that is going through your head pass these qualities? If not, they are not worth thinking about!

Make sure your thoughts are God-honoring. Stay powerful!

- **Helmet of Salvation** – In Ephesians chapter 6, we learn about the full armor of God. The verse I want us to focus on is **Ephesians 6:17** *"Take the helmet of salvation…"* The helmet protects the brain, and our thoughts. In a real battle, a soldier wouldn't think about going into battle without their helmet on. Why? To protect their physical brain. Why should we be any different in our spiritual battles? To get through this crazy life you need that helmet on. The helmet of salvation covers our minds with restorative and redeeming thoughts of our salvation. If we keep our minds on that, we will stay focused, grounded and able to withstand difficulties we face every day.

How do I get that helmet? You already did, it comes with the act of salvation which is asking Christ in your life. You gained so much with that decision but the problem is sometimes we forget or allow that decision to go stale. We forget that we are His, and He is with us. Christ brings us freedom and power. Keeping our decision for Christ fresh, will allow that helmet of salvation to stay on and active and provide our minds with the protection it deserves.

C. Powerful Words

   - Your words are spirit and have creative power. The tongue is a powerful muscle, that is a physiologic truth, but spiritually the tongue also has a lot of power. Scripture gives a ton of warnings about the tongue. Here are a few:
   - ***Proverbs 15:4*** *"The soothing tongue is a tree of life, but a perverse tongue crushes the spirit."*
   - ***Psalms 120:2*** *"Save me, Lord, from lying lips and from deceitful tongues."*
   - ***Psalms 52:2*** *"You who practice deceit, your tongue plots destruction; it is like a sharpened razor."*
   - ***Psalms 64:3"*** *They sharpen their tongues like swords and aim cruel words like deadly arrows."*
   - ***Proverbs 12:19*** *"Truthful lips endure forever, but a lying tongue lasts only a moment."*
   - ***Proverbs 18:21*** *"The tongue has the power of life and death, and those who love it will eat its fruit."*

There are so many more than this. The warnings are clear, if the tongue is used incorrectly, it can be so damaging. On the flip side, the tongue also holds positive qualities as well. Here are some scriptures that discuss that side.
   - ***2 Samuel 23:2*** *"The Spirit of the Lord spoke through me; his word was on my tongue."*
   - ***Psalms 16:9*** *"Therefore my heart is glad and my tongue rejoices; my body also will rest secure."*
   - ***Psalms 35:28*** *"My tongue will proclaim your righteousness, your praises all day long."*
   - ***Proverbs 12:18*** *"The words of the reckless pierce like swords, but the tongue of the wise brings healing."*
   - ***Acts 2:26*** *"Therefore my heart is glad and my tongue rejoices; my body also will rest in hope."*
   - ***Proverbs 15:1*** *"A gentle answer turns away wrath, but a harsh word stirs up anger."*

So, I will say it again, your words are spirit and have creative and destructive power. Use your mouth wisely. A foul mouth is a pitiful mouth, a holy mouth is a powerful mouth and reflects a powerful soul.

- **What you speak you become.** We have already determined that our words are powerful but this is a slightly different perspective. When you speak a negative message to yourself or to others it holds power. It can take root and grow into untruth in their mind and soul. Do you want to be responsible for creating unhealthy soul beliefs in others? I don't think so. Speak power into others. Speak power into yourself. You are inhabited by God almighty, belief it and receive it! I hear people say, "I am no good", "God can never use me", "I am not strong", and so many other negative messages, and they hear it, they believe it and they become it. Not anymore! Remember, we are choosing powerful over pitiful so we are going to speak life into each other and ourselves. God created you. He does not create junk. You are fearfully and wonderfully made- make the words that leave your mouth reflect it!

> ***James 1:26*** *"Those who consider themselves religious and yet do not keep a tight rein on their tongues deceive themselves, and their religion is worthless."*

Chapter 7

Worksheet 1

~ Living the Victorious Life ~

Lesson 7 – Worksheet 1
Living the Victorious Life

1. What does the word victorious mean to you?

    _____
    _____
    _____
    _____

2. List 3 storms that you have endured in your life.

    -   _____
        _____
    -   _____
        _____
    -   _____
        _____

3. Can you list areas that you have grown or lessons that
    you have learned through those storms?

    _____
    _____
    _____
    _____
    _____
    _____
    _____

4. You have accomplished a lot in a short time and I have
    asked you to be brutally honest on most of these
    exercises. I pray that you are feeling victorious. Write
    your thoughts below on where you are at. Are you
    feeling victorious? Why or Why not?

    _____
    _____
    _____
    _____

_____
_____
_____
_____

Write out these verses from our lesson:
- *1 Corinthians 15:57 -*

_____
_____
_____

-Deuteronomy 20:4

_____
_____
_____

-1 John 5:4

_____
_____
_____

Choose your favorite verse from these three and commit it to memory. Write it on a card and put it somewhere where you will see it often. Claim it in your life.

End this lesson with prayer and praise! Thank God for the victories in your life!

Chapter 7

Worksheet 2

~ Powerful Thoughts~

Lesson 7 – Worksheet 2
Powerful Thoughts

1. Would you consider your thought life healthy? Why or why not?

    _____
    _____
    _____
    _____
    _____
    _____
    _____

2. List 6 items that would be unhealthy to spend your time thinking about.

    - _____
    - _____
    - _____
    - _____
    - _____
    - _____

3. Now list 6 items that would be healthy to spend your time thinking about.

    - _____
    - _____
    - _____
    - _____
    - _____
    - _____

4. Now give both lists the whatever test:
- Whatever is true?
- Whatever is noble?
- Whatever is right?
- Whatever is pure?
- Whatever is lovely?
- Whatever is admirable?
- Whatever is excellent or praiseworthy?

5. What did you learn from this exercise?

_____
_____
_____
_____
_____
_____
_____
_____

6. Look up the following verses and write what they teach you about your thought life:
- Psalms 1:2

_____
_____

- Psalms 48:9

_____
_____

- Psalms 77:12

_____
_____

- Romans 13:14

_____
_____

- John 5:39

_____

_____

-Psalms 139:23

_____

_____

-Matthew 9:4

_____

_____

Chapter 7

Worksheet 3

~ Powerful Words ~

Lesson 7 – Worksheet 3
Powerful Words

1. Think about a time that you were hurt by someone else's words. Write about that event here:

   _____

   _____

   _____

   _____

   _____

   _____

   _____

2. How did their words make you feel?

   _____

   _____

   _____

3. Now, on the flipside, write about a time that you hurt someone with your words.

   _____

   _____

   _____

   _____

   _____

   _____

   Back then, you may not have felt bad but now, after our lesson, how do you feel after using those words?

   _____

   _____

   _____

4. Write out *Ephesians 4:29* below:

_____

_____

_____

5. What does this verse tell us not to do?

_____

_____

_____

6. What does it instruct us to do?

_____

_____

_____

7. Now write out *James 3:9-10* below:

_____

_____

_____

_____

_____

_____

8. What does that scripture tell us?

_____

_____

_____

9. For the last part of this worksheet, we are going to practice speaking life into other people. I want you to pick 3 people out and speak positive words over them. Then, write about your experience here. It is amazing what positive words can do!

_____

_____

_____

_____

_____

_____

RRM Snapshot .... Meet Amanda ~

Blessed to have a large and loving family, my childhood was seemingly uneventful from the outside looking in. One area I was lacking was being taught about healthy boundaries. I began looking for love in the wrong places.

While still in high school, I began hanging with older people who were making wrong choices. There was one guy in particular that I ended up spending a lot of time with and as a result the drinking and drugs that he chose, I did as well.

By age 21, I was pregnant with my daughter whose father had been abusive to the point of breaking my nose. Before I knew it, I was a single mother and the pressures started adding up and I resorted to what I knew. I became addicted to prescription meds, Adderall, Xanax and alcohol. To keep up with this addiction and appearances, I had another addiction.... shoplifting.

Three years later, I was pregnant with my son. I had been through 2 broken relationships. The second boyfriend had even held a gun to my head. I had no self-worth and was trying to be a mom, while acting "normal" to family and those around me.

When my son was four, I had been in and out of jail several times. The longest stay was for 10 months and I lost custody of my kids. My shoplifting, alcohol and drug addictions were spiraling and I became hopeless.

September of 2015, just before my 30th birthday, I entered the program at Radical Restoration home for women in Ormond Beach, Florida. God taught me that I was His and I was valuable and I began my journey of renewed self-worth. Through His power and grace, I stopped all of my addictions. I finally had hope!

God has been so faithful. I regained custody of my kids who are now fifteen and 12. I have secured a home for us. I work in management in a local restaurant and have been promoted and am training new employees. None of this would have been possible without the power of God in my life. Even through the unfortunate death of my brother recently, God remained my Rock and the old life remains buried. God can do the same for you! Blessings to you on your journey!

Chapter 8

Walk it Out

~ Staying True ~
~ Give it Away ~

Lesson 8- Walk it Out

Before we start this chapter I want to say how proud I am of you! You have done a lot of work to get to this point! You have surrendered your life to Jesus. You have learned so much about God the Father, the Son and the Holy Spirit. You have learned how God views you and the correct way for you to see your God. You have learned how valuable worship and time with God is. You have identified counterfeits, strongholds, oppressions and unhealthy soul beliefs. You have learned to stay powerful and not pitiful. Now, we are on to the last chapter and this one may be my favorite because we will look how to continue on this amazing journey with our Christ. Then, last but not least we learn to give it away, which means multiplication of souls for the kingdom! That is why we are here, to make Christ known, so let's finish strong!

A. Staying True

To be effective ambassadors for Christ we have to stay true. We need to develop good habits that will keep Christ first, protect our time in God's word and maintain a healthy prayer live. Here are some of my best tips on how to do exactly that.

1. Stay low and glow
The best place you can be is on your knees. Time in prayer is never time wasted. Stay on your face and seek the Lord daily.
> - *1 Thessalonians 5:17* *"Pray continually."*
> - *Ephesians 6:18* *"And pray in the Spirit on all occasions with all kinds of prayers and requests. With this in mind, be alert and always keep on praying for all the Lord's people."*
> - *Romans 8:26* *"In the same way, the Spirit helps us in our weakness. We do not know what we ought to pray for, but the spirit himself intercedes for us through wordless groans."*

- Proverbs 3:5-6 *"Trust in the Lord with all your heart and lean not on your own understanding. In all your ways acknowledge him and he will direct your paths."*

All of these verses reinforce the importance of prayer- and even if we don't know how to pray, the Spirit will help you. So, stay low today and glow away.

2. Godfidence

What is Godfidence? It is a term that I came up with to describe a confidence that you have only when you have God in your life. You see, the power of Christ lives within us so we are not on our own. We have the greatest of allies living within us and we need to walk through each day with that kind of confidence.

- *Galatians 2:20* *"I have been crucified with Christ and I no longer live, but Christ lives in me. The life I now live in the body, I live by faith in the Son of God, who loved me and gave himself for me."*

The you who used to be is no longer. You are now walking with Godfidence and it makes you unstoppable. Claim it and be proud of it!

3. Integrity

My favorite definition for integrity is doing right even when no one is looking. Even the littlest actions matter because the truth of the matter is that people are watching. And even when they are not, Christ always knows not only our behavior but our heart. Our integrity is a direct reflection of our heart. Does this mean we need to be perfect? Of course not, no human is perfect. But we need to strive to do our best and that means making good choices and doing right. Yes, that means honesty at all cost.

- Colossians 3:23 **"Whatever you do, work at it with all your heart, as working for the Lord, not for human masters."*

4. **Truth**

Isn't integrity the same as truth? Not exactly.
Integrity is your honesty, morals and actions all wrapped up
into one. Truth involves no deception, lies or withholding a
secret. Secrets make you sick. Truth requires exposing
everything that is sinful or harmful to you or others. Those
around you deserve the truth. You start to gradually slip in
your relationship with Christ if you are not honest. My
experience is, once someone starts to lie, or hide the fact that
they are struggling, it is a rapid descent into a full-blown
relapse. Do you want to go back to where you came from?
No one ever really wants that. But being less than honest
will get you there. Make a decision today to be honest in all
things.

- *Ephesians 4:25* *"Therefore each of you must put
off falsehood and speak truthfully to your
neighbor, for we are all members of one body."*
- *Colossians 3:9* *"Do not lie to each other, since
you have taken off your old self with its
practices."*

5. S.O.A.P. up!

We all need to be in scripture to walk out our faith
effectively. It is our roadmap, our guidebook and our
encouragement. We truly need it to survive as a Christian in
this fallen world we live in. A good approach to study
scripture is called the SOAP method. It is easy to do,
remember and is effective as well. This is how it works:

S-tudy scripture – Pick a book of the Bible at a time
and work your way through it. You can read a
chapter a day or maybe somedays God will
teach you a lot in a couple verses.

O-bserve what it says – Reading scripture is not a
race. Take time to absorb it. Allow it to permeate
your head and heart.

A-pply- think about how it fits in your life – This is an important aspect. All scripture is applicable but pray about what God is teaching you specifically. As you spend more and more time in the Word you will be amazed what He teaches you.

P-rayer & personalize—Spend time in prayer over what you read. Insert your name into passages. It is meant for you, read it as such. I highly encourage you to journal with your quiet time. Write what God is teaching you. Keep track of prayer requests and how God answers them. It is amazing to look back and see how God has been faithful in your life over time.

This is a great way to start healthy habits of Bible study. You can take a bar of soap but unless you put it on your body it does nothing. Likewise, you can have a Bible but if it sits unread, it does nothing.

> *- 2 Timothy 3:16* *"All scripture is God-breathed and is useful for teaching, rebuking, correcting and training in righteousness."*

6. Radical obedience leads to ridiculous favor

This is one of my favorites! It is so true and incredible too. I have seen this come to fruition so many times in my life. Once I made the decision to live for Christ, the favor of God has been on my life. I have been in financial need on many occasions, only to have God come through in just the way I needed. I have needed rent money, and was down to the last day and someone from the church came by and gave me the exact amount that I owed.

I had my car stolen once and when they found it and returned it, it had a custom tint job done to the windows. Ha! How about that? I have countless stories like this. God can, and will take something bad and turn it to your good if you are faithful and obedient to Him. The key is trusting Him- really, truly trusting him with every aspect of your life! Do you want that favor in your life? Then give him your obedience!

> - *John 14:15* *"If you love me, keep my commands."*
> - *1 John 2:5* *"But if anyone obeys his word, love for God is truly made complete in them. This is how we know we are in him."*

B. Give it Away

Ok, are you ready to share all that you have learned and all that Christ has done for you? I hope so because that is our role on this good green earth. We are to lead others into this incredible journey. God's desire is that no one spends eternity away from Him. Unfortunately, people have their own free will and some will never accept God and His love. But we can certainly give it a try. Here are some tips on giving away the best gift ever:

1. Be laid down lovers of Jesus

Allow the love of Jesus to permeate and navigate your life. If Christ is in first place on your priorities, He will bless you and direct you. He will put you in situations to share His love by action and word. You will find yourself sharing your story to anyone who will listen. Your test has now turned into a testimony and by sharing it with other people, they will want to know how to get the same results. There are so many lost people in the world. Addictions, affairs, abandonment, hopelessness and so many more situations have many searching for answers. We carry that answer!

- *2 Corinthians 1:3-4 "Praise be to God and Father of our Lord Jesus Christ, the Father of compassion and the God of all comfort, who comforts us in all our troubles, to that we can comfort those in any trouble with the comfort we ourselves receive from God."*

2. Don't compromise- people are looking

I have mentioned this before but it is so true. A friend of mine says it this way, "the testimony you live is the greatest testimony you can give." Basically, the way we respond to situations, treat others and even act while driving (I fail on this one too), can encourage others or make them wonder about what a Christian is. Again, we will never be perfect but we can strive to do better every day. Be the person who smiles at the cashier. Be the person who offers a hand to an elderly person or the mother of four who has her hands full. If we respond with anger and rudeness, how are different than the world. If we are cussing and living a promiscuous lifestyle, that does not exude the love of Christ. We are to be lovers of Christ in all situations and at all times.

- *1 Timothy 4:12 Don't let anyone look down on you because you are young, but set an example for the believers in speech, in conduct, in love, in faith, and in purity.*

3. If I'm about His business, He'll be about mine.

What is the business of God? I can think of the top two. First, the great commission is found in *Mark 16:15 "He said to them, "Go into all the world and preach the gospel to all creation."* This is not a suggestion. These are the words of Jesus to His disciples.

Even in these current and uncertain days, we are His disciples and we need to continue this task. Share Christ!

Second, we are commanded to love!

- *John 15:17 "This is my command: love each other."*

- *1 Peter 4:8* *"Above all, love each other deeply, because love covers over a multitude of sins."*
- *John 15:12* *"My command is this: Love each other as I have loved you."*

These two are linked- when we love people through their mess, we share Jesus. I have held many girls as they detox; shaking, puking, and sweating. My husband and I have shared hope to hopeless prisoners. One of my favorite activities is finding homeless people and talking with them, sharing the love of Jesus. I have invited homeless people to stay in my home. What have you done to share the love of Jesus lately?

4. Be a fruit inspector

Another one of my favorites! Our fruit is evidence of our heart. What do you mean by that? Well, a healthy tree produces fruit. A healthy Christian produces fruit too. Our fruit is measured by the number souls saved, and people changed. Read this passage:
- *Matthew 7:16-20* *"By their fruit you will recognize them. Do people pick grapes from thorn bushes, or figs from thistles? Likewise, every good tree bears good fruit, but a bad tree bears bad fruit. A good tree cannot bear bad fruit, and a bad tree cannot bear good fruit. Every tree that does not bear good fruit is cut down and thrown into the fire. Thus, by their fruit you will recognize them."*

Pretty powerful, right? Are you bearing fruit?

Another aspect of fruit inspection is making sure that we are practicing the Fruits of the Spirit. This is a great way to do a daily check on our walk.

- *Galatians 5:22* *But the fruit of the spirit is love, joy, peace, patience, kindness, goodness and faithfulness."*

Is your life showing evidence of these fruits? If not, it is time to start. We are also to called to keep others accountable. We are sisters and brothers in Christ and we need to help each other navigate life in this fallen world. There is no one better to keep us accountable than our fellow believers. If you notice your sister or brother not bearing the fruits of the spirit, you need to gently call them out. It is for their good and the hope is that they would do the same for you. Be a fruit inspector, but do it in love!

- ***Thessalonians 5:11*** *"Therefore encourage one another and build each other up just as in fact you are doing."*

5. Me too ministries

I mentioned this in an earlier lesson but it is worth discussing again. Because I have made so many poor choices in my past life, I can also relate to many women in similar sinful lifestyles. I call it my "Me to ministry." It is common for people to think that no one can understand their pain, but when you have walked a similar road, you can understand and offer empathy. This empathy opens a door for you to share Jesus and what he has done in your life. Don't waste your experiences! Use them for good. You have been healed and are walking in freedom, don't you want to share that with others? Look today for others that you can say, "me too" to!

- ***James 1:2-4*** *"Consider it pure joy my brothers whenever you face trials of many kinds, because you know that the testing of your faith develops perseverance. Perseverance must finish its work so that you may be mature and complete, not lacking anything."*

Use your trials, the perseverance that you have developed and the maturity you have achieved to share Jesus with those around you!

6. Rising up a remnant that's not afraid

The phrase "fear not" is found in scripture 365 times. Do you think that is a coincidence? I don't think so. Every day of the year you can find a different scripture telling you to not be afraid. Why do you think this is? Because Christ wants us to rely fully on him. When we do that, we truly have nothing to fear. This links with our Godfidence, we can be confident that our God loves and cares for us. Share this Godfidence as we raise up a remnant that is growing in size.

We have a passion inside of us, a fire! A fire is hard to ignore and easy to spread. This is one fire that you want to spread. Let your sparks touch those around you. Let the fire of Christ's love grow hot inside of you!

To close out this chapter I want you to read
Hebrews 12:1-2a:
"Therefore, since we are surrounded by such a great cloud of witnesses, let us throw off everything that hinders and the sin that so easily entangles. And let us run with perseverance the race marked out for us, fixing our eyes on Jesus, the pioneer and perfecter of faith. "

This is our calling- we have the most amazing gift and freedom and we are to give it away. Do your part and share Jesus with all those who will listen. Don't waste what God has given you, let's multiply and give it away!

Chapter 8

Worksheet 1

~ Staying True ~

Lesson 8 – Worksheet 1
Staying True

Since we started with prayer on this lesson, that is where we begin
with this worksheet. Take some time to go before your God and
thank Him for where He has brought you, worship Him for who He is
and ask Him to be with you for these exercises.

Write out **Ephesians 6:18** here:

_____

_____

_____

_____

1. How would you rate your confidence from 1-10? Why?

    _____

    _____

    _____

    _____

2. Now that you have Godfidence how do you see that
    changing? _____

    _____

    _____

    _____

3. Integrity and honesty- Write about a time where you failed
    in these areas:

    _____

    _____

    _____

    _____

    _____

    _____

    _____

4. Ok- now we are going to start our good habits by starting studying the Bible using SOAP. You will need a journal or something to write on. Here are the instructions from the lesson again. Write them in your journal or tape this into it. Enjoy digging in and having intimate time in God's Word.

> **S-tudy scripture** – Pick a book of the Bible at a time and work your way through it. You can read a chapter a day or maybe somedays God will teach you a lot in a couple verses.
> **O-bserve what it says** – Reading scripture is not a race. Take time to absorb it. Allow it to permeate your head and heart.
> **A-pply- think about how it fits in your life** – This is an important aspect. All scripture is applicable but pray about what God is teaching you specifically. As you spend more and more time in the Word you will be amazed what he teaches you.
> **P-rayer & personalize**—Spend time in prayer over what you read. Insert your name into passages. It is meant for you, read it as such. I highly encourage you to journal with your quiet time. Write what God is teaching you. Keep track of prayer requests and how God answers them. It is amazing to look back and see how God has been faithful in your life over time.

5. **Radical Obedience**- what does that phrase mean to you personally? I want you to write a few sentences answering that question.

_____

_____

_____

_____

_____

_____

_____

Chapter 8

Worksheet 2

~ Give it Away ~

Lesson 8 – Worksheet 2
Giving it Away

1. Make a list of family members and friends that you can share Christ with:

   - _____
   - _____
   - _____
   - _____
   - _____
   - _____
   - _____
   - _____

These will not be the only people you share Jesus with but they may be the hardest. Reaching those close to us takes courage but we want them in heaven with us for sure. So, be in prayer about your list and pray also for opportunities to share and for their hearts to be open.

2. Review the fruits of the Spirit Love, Joy, Peace, Patience, Kindness, Goodness, Gentleness, Faithfulness, and Self-Control. Now I want you to do some soul seeking and write which 3 you are strongest at:

   1. _____
   2. _____
   3. _____

3. Which 3 are you weakest at:

   1. _____
   2. _____
   3. _____

4. Make a plan here on how you can improve in these areas:

_____
_____
_____
_____
_____
_____
_____

5. For the "Me-to" Ministry you need to be aware of what you can offer. Make a list here of what you can offer to others from your past. In other words, what have you gone through that you help others with.

        1. _____

        2. _____

        3. _____

        4. _____

        5. _____

        6. _____

Close with prayer- worship Him and thank Him for finishing this curriculum. Now get to changing the world for Christ. Praise Him for your Radical Restoration and help others do the same! Blessings to you!

*** All scripture references are NIV unless noted otherwise.

*** All RRM testimonies are printed will full permission of each of the persons that allowed us to share their stories. Thank you to each of them for their candid and accurate testimonies!

Contact Information

Dr. Dawn Knighton Adkins ~
Radical Restoration Ministries

To read Dawn's complete story, go to amazon.com and purchase "Radical Restoration- The Dawn Knighton Story"

For more information on Radical Restoration Ministries and Dr. Dawn Adkins, please go to RadicalRestorationMinistries.com. You can also like Radical Restoration Ministries on Facebook.

To contact the ministry for speaking engagements, consulting, training seminars on residential rehabilitation programs or for placement: RadicalRestorationMinistries@gmail.com

To donate to the ministry please go to our website.

RADICAL RESTORATION MINISTRIES

Tawnya M. Shaffer

To read another of Tawnya's books, go to amazon.com and order "Words from Birds." It is a collection of 60 pertinent, daily devotions about the attributes of the eagle and other birds that share comparisons with our human nature.

Tawnya is an author and speaker. She is available to speak to women's groups, youth and children's groups and camps. Her desire is to use her past to give hope to all ages.

Contact her @
tawnya.radicalrestoration@gmail.com

She is in process on two other non-fiction books that will offer hope and instruction for our daily walk with Christ. Feel free to connect with her to be added to her mailing list on new releases.

Made in the USA
Middletown, DE
06 March 2022

62226617R00146